VEGETARIAN NIRVANA

A PASSAGE TO NORTH INDIAN CUISINE

By

Santosh Jain

To Jill.
with best wishes
Santosh Jain

ISBN: 1-4140-0917-8 (e-book)
ISBN: 1-4140-0916-X (Paperback)

Library of Congress Control Number: 2003097254

This book is printed on acid free paper.

Printed in the United States of America
Bloomington, IN

1stBooks - rev. 10/13/03

Acknowledgments

Vegetarian Nirvana is the result of an effort that started some twenty years ago. It is the outcome of a process of experimentation, turbulences of trial and error, and a lot of help in the form of suggestions from friends and relatives.

The initial encouragement came from my dear friend Prema Popkin, whose cooperation inspired confidence in me to undertake such an arduous venture. But with the demands of work and family, my initial enthusiasm (to say nothing of my energy level) did not last very long and I almost gave up on the project. However, when I was asked to give cooking lessons to friends at my home, and at the insistence of those who attended the classes, that I should write a book, my enthusiasm resurfaced. In particular, when Judith Granbois offered her services for computerizing and editing my recipes, this project began anew. I am grateful to her for her contribution in giving shape to this work. The process continued with encouragement coming from various quarters.

Without the help of my family, namely, my dear husband, Chaman, who made excellent contributions in the organization and formatting of the book, our son Manu, who suggested the title for the book and our daughter Madhulika, who experimented following my recipes and provided valuable feedback, this book would not have been possible. The Kashmiri recipes were the result of my niece Sunalini's suggestions and contributions. Through the years, cooking lessons I gave in the form of classes provided me with opportunities to ask for and receive comments and suggestions from my students. Their suggestions have often proven to be most valuable.

Santosh Jain   August 1, 2003
Bloomington, Indiana

Table of Contents

    Sabut Masar (Whole Brown Lentils or Flageolets)
    Gajjar Bhaji (Dry-cooked Carrots)
    Bhindi Bhaji (Dry-cooked Okra)
    Plain Rice or Chapatis

    Masoor Dal aur Sabzi (Masoor Dal with Vegetables)
    Panch Pooran Alu (Potatoes with Panch Pooran)
    Plain Rice

    Dhuli Moong Dal (Washed Moong Dal)
    Alu Baigan Bhaji (Eggplant and Potatoes)
    Raita with Cucumbers and Tomatoes
    Chapatis

Introduction

I have written this book to teach the basics of Indian vegetarian cooking for the home cook. The recipes are designed to create meals that are healthy, appealing and delicious. I have drawn from my experience in the kitchen to develop the recipes and the methods and techniques reflect the way I like to do things in the kitchen. I begin by offering practical instruction to provide a firm grasp of the fundamentals. Once you have mastered the basic techniques, you can explore the many and varied menus for guidance on your culinary journeys into some of the varied cuisines of India.

The book has three main objectives:

First, I have written the recipes as a series of menus that progress from those that are easy and relatively quick to prepare and move on to more challenging dishes that build on techniques you will have already learned. The first several menus begin with basic, day-to-day cooking. The later menus are often meals that are prepared for entertaining and festive occasions. As you become familiar with Indian spices and cooking techniques, don't be afraid to try more the more complex menus and continue to improve your grasp of Indian cuisine. Eventually, you will be able to compose your own menus.

Second, these recipes rely on ingredients that are readily available in the supermarket and utensils that are familiar to American cooks. I have provided alternatives where recipes include a few ingredients that are found only in Asian food markets. You may start out using the substitutes and get satisfactory results. Because Indian cooking is basically a top-of-the-stove cooking, an experienced cook should have all the necessary tools. A beginner may need to get a few additions, such as a wok or a small rolling pin. I will discuss utensils in more detail in the Techniques section.

Third, my menus are designed to provide balanced meals - nutritionally balanced, of course, but also balanced to provide contrasting tastes and textures and to appeal to the senses. If you cook a basic dal, the accompanying vegetable should have complementary seasoning and texture. The meal is completed with rice or bread (or sometimes both), depending on the availability of time and resources. Some dals taste better with rice than chapatis (such as Masoor Dal); others (e.g., Urd Dal) definitely taste better with chapatis. In North India, the region from which nearly all of these recipes come, chapatis are a staple and are served with every meal, while rice is optional. Yogurt, chutney, a little salad, papadum, and pickles are enhancements to a typical North Indian meal.

How I learned to cook

In my family of five sisters and one brother, there was no question of liking or disliking - we simply had to learn to cook. Like my other sisters, I had always helped my mother with stirring or simple preparations, but unlike the others, there was something in me that wanted to learn more. My love of cooking struck me at the age of eleven, and I began experimenting in the kitchen when my mother wasn't home. The first dish I remember making was halvah, which turned out quite well. By the time I was twelve, I was helping to cook three or four meals a week. During this period, my mother taught me the 'basics' of north Indian cooking.

The first thing most young girls in North India learn to make is a chapati, a kind of basic, flat Indian bread. To be considered eligible for marriage, a girl must make a perfectly round chapati. Soon after the wedding, an Indian bride is initiated in her in-laws' kitchen by cooking a simple dish for her father-in-law, who rewards her with a token gift of money or jewelry. My in-law must have been skeptical about my husband's city bride. On our first visit to my husband's parents' home, my mother-in-law announced, "Tomorrow is the day." "And," she continued, "we have invited three families for lunch." I had never cooked for such a large group before, but I managed to produce pooris, two vegetables and halva. Apparently, I passed the test.

Raised as a Jain, an ancient Indian religious tradition, I was taught to cook according to the principles of Jainism. Jain teaching prohibits killing animals and eating foods with meat in them. This rule can be interpreted so stringently that many Jains don't eat root vegetable or any food that even resembles meat. In our household growing up, we did not use garlic, onions, or even fresh ginger, and we used only limited amounts of tomatoes, because of their resemblance to meat. Thus, the major foods eaten in my home were rice, dals, breads and vegetables.

Growing up, we did not plan meals in advance as many families do here in the United States. The daily morning visit to the market decided the menus for the noon and evening meals each day. The noon meal usually consisted of a vegetable with gravy, a dry vegetable, yogurt and chapatis; the evening meal featured a dry vegetable, dal, rice and chapatis. For breakfast during the week, we had milk with toast or paratha, another delicious Indian bread. Breakfast was more elaborate on the weekends, perhaps consisting of stuffed parathas, halvah or vermicelli with milk.

After my marriage in 1961, I was on my own. Free to use whatever ingredients and techniques I wished, I started to experiment with different dishes and new flavors. If I encountered a tasty Bengali or Gujarati dish (my family is Punjabi) or learned of an interesting technique, I incorporated it into my cooking.

I moved to Bloomington, Indiana, in 1970 with my husband and two children, and my cooking repertoire expanded to encompass a vast range of ingredients and cuisines. After a few years in the United States had passed, I was asked to give cooking demonstrations and to share my country's cuisine. Since then I have continued to offer Indian cooking classes at various locations, including in my own kitchen for the past few years.

Why Indian cooking?

I have wondered this myself, as I have been asked more and more often to teach Indian cooking over the years. Americans over the last twenty years have become far more sophisticated in their tastes and more interested in many types of world cuisine. But I also think it is at least partly because of Americans' increasing interest in eating less meat, and incorporating more legumes into their daily diet. For that objective, Indian cooking offers real benefits.

First, despite the rich sauces you may have encountered in Indian restaurants, Indian cuisine properly prepared is healthy. Indian cooks have learned how to combine vegetables, pulses and legumes, and dairy products to take advantage of their complementary proteins, producing delicious food that is also low in cholesterol. They emphasize the importance of using perfectly fresh vegetables and cooking them artfully to preserve their vitamin content.

Second, as one of the world's great cuisines, Indian food is delicious. Developed over thousands of years, it stresses fresh ingredients and sophisticated, custom-blended mixtures of spices and seasonings that subtly enhance flavor.

Third, Indian food is flexible. Some people assume that they will not enjoy it because it is "too hot." The heat, however, is in the hands of the cook. You can produce food that suits your palate. And my recipes not only use a wide range of vegetables but include many suggestions for substitutions. If you don't like cauliflower, for example, you may substitute another vegetable as recommended.

About this cookbook

In writing this cookbook, I decided that the most logical way to present my recipes is to use the approach I have adopted for my cooking classes - to organize the recipes into suggested menus. In this cookbook, the individual recipes for vegetable dishes and dals are found after the menus in which they appear. To avoid repetition, however, dishes that may appear in more than one menu (such as rice, raitas, breads and desserts) are located in separate chapters of their own. The menus begin with basic techniques and limited ingredients and progress to more elaborate preparations. Try a simple menu first. You will learn to cook simple Indian food with exciting flavors. As you become more familiar with ingredients and techniques, you will want to explore the more complicated menus.

Although I am North Indian, I have incorporated techniques and dishes from the varied regions of India. You will find feasts from Punjab, Kashmir, Delhi and other exotic locales. Experience the wonderful culinary treasures from these regions and discover their local flavors. I hope you will enjoy preparing Indian food and sharing it with family and friends.

Utensils

I learned to cook using the most traditional and primitive tools and implements. We ground our spices with a mortar and pestle, and we made our dough by hand. We cooked on an *anghithi*, a small, clay-covered stove that used soft and hard coke for fuel. Each morning, we built a fire in the stove; once lit, it could not be turned on and off. Cooking had to be planned and timed carefully. Dishes that required higher temperatures were cooked first, when the stove was hot; dishes that had to be cooked for a longer time at lower temperatures, like many dals, were put on the stove later. The whole process had to be repeated for the evening meal. The stove was inconvenient and frustrating to use. Since this rather short stove sat on the floor, my sisters and I had to cook sitting on the floor with the smoke blowing in our eyes.

More than any other job in the kitchen, I hated breaking up the coke, which came in big chunks, to make pieces that fit the stove. The job always left my hands black. If it rained, the coke got wet, and the effort to light the stove became a soggy, smoky nightmare. I used to bribe my younger sisters with promises of their favorite foods, or failing that, threaten them with bodily harm to take on that job for me. I also managed to similarly persuade them to make the dough for chapatis, another chore I particularly disliked (thank goodness for the heavy duty mixer—my younger sisters are no longer nearby!).

We even prepared our own grains for grinding into flour, although, unlike many families, we did not have to use a hand-cranked mill for the job. About every two weeks, my mother, sisters and I would wash our whole wheat grains, dry them, clean them and take the whole lot to the *chakki* (the local neighborhood miller) to be milled. We had to be careful to keep bugs out of our food, storing everything in containers with air-tight lids.

During the monsoon, the constant moisture caused even bigger problems in purchasing, storing and preparing food. At that season, many Jain families ate fewer fresh vegetables, because they tended to have more undetected insects during the monsoon months (in the Jain tradition, eating an animal even unintentionally is considered a sin).

With the memories of those crude kitchen arrangements in mind, I must admit that today, I really enjoy using the Cuisinart, the blender, the slow cooker, the pressure cooker, the electric coffee grinder and every other modern convenience.

As to your kitchen, there are some basic utensils that are essential, while others are helpful, but optional. Because Indian cooking is primarily top-of-the-stove cooking, the quality of your pots and pans is very important. All of my recipes have been developed for use with heavy-duty, nonstick pots and pans. For Indian and any other cuisine, I highly recommend that you invest in a good set of pots and pans.

Using heavy cookware offers several advantages. Once a heavy pan has been heated to the desired temperature, you can reduce the heat as specified in the recipes. Low heat cooks the dish more evenly, and you don't have to add extra moisture, particularly in cooking vegetables. Vegetables cooked on low heat in their own juices are a lot more flavorful.

Nonstick coatings are additionally useful, because you can use less fat. If you are not using nonstick pans, then you may need to increase the amount of oil called for in the recipes.

Most of the pots and pans I use will be familiar to Western cooks. A griddle or cast-iron skillet can be used to make chapatis or parathas. A wok is essential for deep frying. An Indian *karahi* is shaped a little differently than a wok, but a wok is fine for deep frying.

The only thing brought from India that I use in my cooking is a rolling pin. My Indian rolling pin is small, about 6 inches long, and carved out of a single piece of wood. You can use a Western-style rolling pin, but I prefer my old one.

Ingredients

When I first came to the United States, finding ingredients was quite a challenge. There were almost no dals available in the supermarket, except for black-eyed peas, kidney beans and split peas (even finding brown lentils was a challenge!). Chick pea flour and gram flour were unheard of. Even the vegetable selection was somewhat limited, and farmer's markets weren't that prevalent. I had to use some ingenuity to come up with substitutes for foods essential to dessert making that were familiar to me but unavailable in the United States, like panir, rabri and khoya.

Today, Americans are much more cosmopolitan in their diet, enjoying a vast range of foods from all over the world. Today's cooks can find many of the ingredients they need for Indian cooking right at the local supermarket, filling in with purchases from international food stores or mail order sources. And farmers' markets, once a small phenomenon in limited locales, have opened all over the country, providing wonderful fresh produce in season.

One item that is not available even now is *khoya*, a dairy product that is sold in bricks in India. Good khoya should be creamy but a little grainy. Initially, I tried cooking down a mixture of powdered milk and half and half, but the product was too sticky and too smooth. Eventually, I tried combining *panir* (home made cheese) with powdered milk and half and half, and that combination succeeded.

Spices

There is a common misunderstanding in the West that all Indian food is hot, but "spicy" and "hot". The degree of heat can be varied according to individual tastes: the cook is in control.

One concept that I try to emphasize to my students is that a "hot" dish is one where one spice, usually cayenne pepper, is the predominant flavor and the dish often sets your mouth on fire without letting you taste the food. A "spicy" dish, on the other hand, is one where the flavor comes from a combination of several spices, which may or may not include cayenne. In this kind of dish, the spices complement the main flavors, rather than overwhelm them.

In some dishes contain the same spice in two different forms - whole and ground. The two versions differ quite a bit in flavor (coriander seeds and fresh coriander, for example, taste nothing like each other).

Indian cooking uses many spices that are familiar to American cooks, such as cinnamon, cloves and black pepper. Others may require a little explanation.

Ajwain is another name for lovage. Ajwain looks something like celery seeds. It is used whole, but somewhat sparingly, because of its strong flavor.

Amchur powder is made from ground, dried raw mango. Its taste is tart or sour. If you cannot find it, you may substitute lemon juice, tomatoes or sour yogurt, as recommended in individual recipes.

Asafoetida is a dried resin that comes from the roots of plants. It is available in lump or ground form. Its strong flavor is definitely an acquired taste, and it may be omitted from any recipe if you don't like it.

Bay leaf is often added to rice or bean dishes.

Cardamom comes in black, green or white pods. Sometimes the whole pod is used, as in Rice with Whole Spices; sometimes the seeds are removed. Black cardamom, the hardest to find, may be available only in Indian grocery stores, and is primarily used for garam masala.

Chilies Recipes in this book may call for several kinds of chilies. Jalapeño chilies are dark green, elongated but round in shape and about 1 1/2 to 2 inches long. Green cayenne chilies are thin and 3 to 4 inches long. Both are used fresh. Dried red chilies are dark red and about 1 1/2 to 2 inches long. They are used whole or, if you want a hotter dish, broken in half. Many people like to remove them before serving the dish. Used fresh, dried whole or ground, all are available at supermarkets or Indian food stores. The seeds are the hottest part of a chili. They can be removed if you don't want so much heat.

Cilantro is the leaf of the coriander plant. Cilantro is sometimes called green or fresh coriander; I will use the term "cilantro" to avoid confusion. It looks somewhat like Italian or flat leaf parsley, but its flavor is more pungent. In addition to Indian cooking, it is used in Latin American and Chinese dishes and is widely available. It is easy to grow from seed if you have a garden. Cilantro is widely used for garnishes and chutneys and in vegetable dishes or curries.

Cinnamon is used in stick form in rice dishes and in powdered form in garam masala.

Cloves appear whole in rice dishes and in powdered form in garam masala.

Coconut To avoid the labor of cracking the hard shell of a coconut and grating the white flesh, I use finely shredded, unsweetened coconut, available at Indian grocery stores or health food stores.

Coriander seeds are round, beige seeds a little smaller than peppercorns. Coriander is a very common flavor in Indian cooking. My recipes often call for whole roasted coriander seeds, but both whole and ground coriander may appear in a single recipe.

Cumin seeds look like caraway seeds. They come in whole or ground form and, like coriander, are often roasted.

Curry is a term that describes a dish with gravy. There is no plant that is ground up to make curry powder; curry powder is not found in Indian kitchens and is not used in my recipes.

Fennel seeds are green and slightly larger than cumin seeds. They taste like licorice. Fennel seeds and ground fennel are used in panch pooran, chutney and pickles, and some vegetable dishes. Kashmiri cuisine characteristically uses ground fennel with ground ginger.

Fenugreek seeds are small, hard and angular; they lend a distinctive aroma and bitter taste to foods. One of the components of panch pooran, they are also used in pickles. In South India, ground fenugreek appears in many dishes, particularly with sambar or rasam and in whole form in pumpkin or potatoes dishes.

Garam masala is a mixture of spices always added to a dish at the last minute. Every household has its own favorite recipe. Here is mine:

4 tablespoons ground black pepper	1 teaspoon ground cloves
1 tablespoon ground ginger	1 teaspoon ground nutmeg
1 tablespoon ground cinnamon	1 teaspoon ground black or green cardamom

Mix the spices together and store the mixture in a dark, dry place. Garam masala will keep a month on the shelf or 2-3 months in the refrigerator. You can use the whole spices and grind them yourself in a coffee grinder.

Garlic normally is not used by vegetarians. I use garlic in some dishes, but it may be omitted.

Ghee is clarified butter. If you don't have ghee or don't want to make it, you can substitute vegetable oil, peanut oil or butter. [*See page 10 for preparation of ghee.*]

Ginger is used both fresh and dried. Ginger root is a brown, knobby root that is peeled, grated or chopped and used primarily in dals and curries. Its taste is stronger than dried, ground ginger. Ground ginger is thought to reduce flatulence and therefore appears in many dals.

Kalonji (nigella) are small, shiny black seeds, usually used in pickles and panch pooran or sprinkled over naan. If you cannot find them, omit them from the recipe.

Mint is used in green chutneys, seasoning for some raitas and in stuffed parathas.

Mustard seeds come in three varieties - yellow, brown and black. When these recipes call for mustard, you will usually use the black variety. The seeds are smaller than the yellow ones and do not taste as strong. Whole mustard seeds are used in many dishes, where they lend a nutty taste. Pungent ground mustard often appears in pickles.

Nutmeg is the dried seed of a pear-like, yellow-brown fruit. It has a warm, sweet taste and is used ground in garam masala.

Onions are used in curried dishes, vegetables and dals, and they often appear in baghars. Many vegetarians do not use onions in cooking.

Panch pooran is a mixture of five whole spices:

2 teaspoons cumin seeds	1 teaspoon fenugreek seeds
2 teaspoons mustard seeds	1 teaspoon kalonji
2 teaspoons fenne	l seeds

Mix the spices together. Panch pooran can be kept for 4-5 months on the shelf.

Sesame Seeds give certain dishes a nutty taste.

Tamarind comes from a pulp that surrounds the seeds of a tree in the pea family; tamarind seed pods look like big, woody beans. It has a very tart taste. Tamarind pods are available in supermarkets; usually the outer shell is missing and so are many of the seeds. It also comes in dried, half-pound cakes or bottled in paste form. I prefer to use the cakes to make my own pulp. Tamarind is used in a lot of bean dishes, and tamarind chutney is very popular.

To prepare tamarind pulp, rinse a cake of tamarind and soak it in 2 ½ cups hot water for 3-4 hours or until it becomes soft and workable. You will be able to see that it plumps up as it absorbs the water. Mash it with your fingers until it becomes pulpy. Drain it through a colander to separate the pulp from the seeds and stems. (You may get some more pulp out of the seeds and stems by repeating the process and adding a little more water.) Use it immediately. If you wish to keep it, add 1 teaspoon of salt to the pulp and bring it to a boil. Let it cool to room temperature and store in a clean jar. Given this treatment, it will keep for 2-3 weeks in the refrigerator or indefinitely in the freezer.

Turmeric is a ginger-like root but smaller and darker orange. Dried and ground, it gives many Indian foods a golden color. It is considered to be an antiseptic. You can find it dried and ground into a fine powder or occasionally in its fresh, root form. Nearly all of these recipes call for the powder.

Cooking techniques

Baghar is the finishing step for a dal. Baghars are unique to Indian cooking. Adding spices to hot oil or ghee produces a beautiful aroma. The mixture brings out a very different flavor in dal. Many cooks use asafoetida in their baghars; other spices often included are cumin seed, mustard seed, cayenne and garam masala. Sometimes finely chopped onions and tomatoes are also part of the baghar. Once the baghar is prepared, it is poured over the dal and stirred in.

Bhaji is a term that refers to a vegetable that has been cooked "dry", i.e., without a sauce. To cook vegetables in this style, heat oil in a heavy skillet on medium high. Add whole spices (panch pooran, cumin, mustard and asafoetida), ground turmeric and the vegetable. Cover tightly and cook for 5 to 7 minutes on low heat. Many cookbooks call for water to be added, but I prefer to cook the vegetables in their own juices. If the dish contains too much liquid, turn up the heat and cook it off. The vegetables should be tender but should hold their shape.

Bhunao is a cooking technique in which certain foods, such as potatoes or okra, are cooked until they are almost done and then sautéed very slowly on low heat. *Masaledar alu* is an example of the use of this technique.

Curry masala is a gravy that includes specific ingredients. To make a basic curry masala, heat the oil on medium in a pan with a heavy base. Add cumin seeds; they will quickly begin to sizzle and darken. Add ground onions, ginger and garlic and sauté until the color turns light brown. When you stir the vegetables into the oil, the mixture will be homogeneous. After it has cooked for a time, you will see the oil begin to separate from the vegetables. It seems to ooze out of the mixture and to appear around the edges of the vegetables. When the oil begins to separate, stir in turmeric, paprika, cayenne, ground cumin and ground coriander. Add chopped tomatoes and cook, stirring occasionally. As the moisture begins to cook out of the tomatoes, stir frequently and then constantly until the oil again starts to separate. This technique provides the base for a North Indian curry.

Dals In Hindi, "dal" is a generic term, referring to beans or legumes; dals may be whole, or they may have been hulled or put through a mill that splits them. Dals are divided into categories by their form. *Whole dals* include whole moong (mung beans, the small green beans which produce bean sprouts), whole masoor (small gray or brown lentils), whole grams (which look like small very dark brown chick peas), etc. *Split dals* may or may not retain their skins, depending on the variety. Split dals that are most often used are moong dal and urd dal (the same size as moong dal but white). Familiar *washed and split dals* include chana dal, masoor dal (pink lentils), moong dal, urd dal, masoor dal and toovar arhar dal (pigeon peas). Other dals are *lobia* (black-eyed peas), *rajmah* (red kidney beans), *kabuli chana* (chick peas) and *kala chana* (black gram). Cooking techniques vary according to the category of dal (i.e., whole, split, washed and split). Split and washed dals should be soaked for at least an hour or two. Whole and hulled dals can be cooked after washing. Other whole beans should be soaked overnight to cut down the cooking time. The key to producing a delicious dal begins with bringing the dal and water to a boil. When the dal is boiling vigorously, reduce the heat to bring the dal to a low boil (more than a simmer and less than rapid boil) and cook until it is tender, but the dal and water are still separate. Then reduce the heat to low and simmer the dal slowly until the mixture thickens and takes on an even consistency. The final step is to add the baghar.

Dry roasting spices Heat a heavy griddle. Do not add oil. Roast the whole spices over medium heat in the dry pan and stir them off occasionally, until they darken and give off their fragrance. Cool them completely and grind them in a coffee grinder.

Ghee [purified butter]: Use a 1- or 2-quart saucepan with a heavy bottom. Melt 1 pound of unsalted butter on low heat. It will melt quickly and will then begin cooking. You will see white solids settle at the bottom of the pan. Continue to cook the butter for 10 to 15 minutes until the moisture has cooked out. It should be a clear yellow liquid. Remove the pan from the heat and let it cool down a bit. Drain the melted butter through a tea strainer or a piece of muslin, discarding the white solids. Once ghee has thoroughly cooled, it solidifies. You can keep ghee at room temperature for at least two weeks and in the refrigerator for 2 months.

Dahi [yogurt]: To make yogurt, boil 1 quart milk in a 3-quart saucepan or in the microwave. It takes about 10-12 minutes to boil a quart of milk in the microwave. When the milk has reached a full boil, remove it from the heat and let it cool down until it is comfortable to the touch. The temperature should be 90-95° F in the winter or 80-85° F in the summer.

Put 2 tablespoons yogurt in a glass jar or glass or pyrex bowl. Smear the yogurt over the bottom and sides of the jar. Pour the boiled milk into the jar and stir well. Cover the jar and wrap it with a small blanket or heavy towel. In the summer, let it sit on the counter. It should take eight to ten hours; letting it sit overnight works well. Refrigerate until needed.

Some recipes call for sour yogurt. To sour the yogurt, let it sit at room temperature for an additional 24 hours.

Panir: To prepare panir take

1/4 cup cold water
1 gallon whole or 2% milk
1/2 cup Realemon lemon juice or 2-3 tablespoons fresh lemon juice

Pour the water into a heavy 6-quart saucepan. The water will help prevent the milk from scorching. Add the milk. Turn the heat to medium high and bring to a boil. Stir the milk after it heats up to dissipate the pressure and reduce the chance of the milk boiling over. As the milk begins to boil, it will rise. As soon as the milk rises, add the lemon juice and stir. The curds will separate from the whey. The whey should be clear. If it is still milky, add a little more lemon juice until you get the desired result. Turn the heat off.

Line a strainer or colander with a double layer of cheesecloth. (If you want to save the whey, place the strainer over a large bowl or pot. Reserved whey can be used for cooking rice if you plan to cook rice the same day.) Pour the curdled milk into the strainer and drain the curds. Gather up the corners of the cheesecloth and twist it to collect the panir, wringing out as much of the whey as you can.

Note: Whenever you are cooking milk, it is helpful to put a wire rack on the burner before you put on the pot. This precaution helps to prevent the milk solids from sticking to the bottom of the pot. Use this technique when making panir, rabri and yogurt.

Hanging the Panir Suspend the cheesecloth with the panir from the faucet and let it drip into the sink for two hours. The panir can be crumbled easily for use in desserts or dishes such as Khoya Matar and can be measured in a measuring cup.

Weighting the Panir When a recipe calls for panir that is cut into cubes, it must be weighted right away. Open the cheesecloth and mold or pat the panir to make a rectangle or square. Fold the cheesecloth over the panir and place it between two cutting boards. Place a large pot filled with water or other weight on top. This step is meant to squeeze the remaining liquid out of the panir, ensuring that the finished panir will be smooth. Let the panir remain under the weight for two to three hours. Remove the slab of panir from the cheesecloth. It is now ready to be cut into cubes and fried. Wrapped in Saran Wrap and refrigerated for later use, it will keep for a couple of days. Use caution in handling hot panir.

Frying the Panir Heat about 2 cups of oil in a wok or deep skillet. Make sure that the oil is hot every time you fry a fresh batch of panir. The cubes of panir should be fried in small batches, taking just enough time for the outside to become golden brown, while the inside remains soft. When the oil is hot enough, the outside will brown quickly. Be careful! Any residual water still in the panir may pop while the cubes are in the oil.

Remove each batch of fried panir cubes and place them in a strainer or colander. After you have fried all of the panir, bring water to boil in a pot just large enough to hold all of the panir. Add 1 teaspoon of salt and the panir cubes. Turn the heat off and let the panir soak for about 30 minutes before adding it to the dish you are preparing. This extra step ensures that the panir will be soft.

The fried panir can be reserved for future use. Panir will keep for three to four days; frozen, it will keep for a couple of months. Soak the frozen panir in boiling water just before you add it to the dish.

Helpful Hints

Make sure the boiling milk has curdled completely and that the whey is clear. Be sure to extract all the liquid from the panir.

Fry the panir cubes in oil only for as long as necessary to brown them lightly on the outside.

Soak the fried panir in boiling salted water for at least 30 minutes to ensure that it will be soft.

If a recipe requires panir made from 1 quart of milk, it is more efficient to make a gallon of panir and reserve the remainder for future use.

Khoya: is solidified milk, which is used for sweets. To make khoya, you will need: Panir made from ½ gallon whole milk, hung and drained 1 quart half and half.

The panir should be hung to drain in the sink until all the excess moisture has dripped out. Crumble the panir with your fingers or in the food processor, using the rubber blade.

Heat the half and half on medium high in a heavy, nonstick skillet for about ten minutes, until it cooks down a little, stirring frequently. Stir in the crumbled panir and continue cooking the mixture, stirring frequently to prevent burning, until the mixture begins to thicken; the process will take about 30 minutes. The thickened paste product is called khoya. As the khoya cools, it will thicken further.

Rabri, thickened half and half without panir, is used in some desserts. To prepare rabri, put a rack on the burner. Pour 2 tablespoons cold water into a heavy skillet. Add 1 quart half and half and heat it on medium high stirring frequently until it is thick and creamy. When it is finished, it should have the consistency of condensed milk.

Menus

Menu Planning

A vegetarian Indian meal is not planned around a main entree with side dishes. Instead, each dish complements the others in a meal, and, what is more, a dal or a curry alone cannot provide nutritional balance. If you decide to serve a dal, you should also cook a vegetable. Rice and/or chapatis provide carbohydrates, while yogurt soothes the stomach. Pickles and chutneys are added according to personal taste.

In India, menu planning usually takes place during a trip to the market. Menus tend to be governed by the choice of vegetables that are available in a given season. Even now, with so much available year round, I still like to use seasonal vegetables and fruits. Oranges may be available in July, but they won't be as good as the ones you can buy in January. Besides, emphasizing the use of seasonal vegetables brings variety to the diet. During the winter, I like to use green, leafy vegetables such as spinach, mustard greens or kohlrabi greens, along with cauliflower, carrots and daikon. During the summer, I look for zucchini, okra and eggplant.

The Indian cook shops for the freshest vegetables available at the peak of their season, building the menu around the vegetable selection. If she finds zucchini, for example, she will consider a second vegetable that contrasts. If she plans to serve the zucchini for lunch in a curry, she might purchase cauliflower for a bhaji or dry vegetable dish. She would not serve zucchini and milk gourd in the same meal, or even on the same day, because they are too similar. She might think about which dal would complement her vegetable for the evening meal. If she plans to serve a dry vegetable, she might choose a creamy dal. If she is serving a dry dal, she might choose to serve it with yogurt or a vegetable prepared with a little sauce. So her noon menu might feature a cauliflower bhaji, served with zucchini and tomatoes, yogurt and chapatis; the evening meal might be spinach or eggplant, served with a carrot bhaji.

In addition to the various vegetable dishes, dals or bean dishes are a very important part of a vegetarian meal, providing the protein needed for a balanced diet. They also contribute a distinct taste and texture to the vegetable dishes in the menu. I created some of the dal recipes in this book for the American kitchen to take advantage of beans that are not available in India.

Preparing several dishes at once can be a daunting task, especially when you are cooking a new cuisine. In this book, I will describe to you in some detail how I might prepare a meal to give you an idea of how to organize your time efficiently. Suppose the menu consists of a dal, a vegetable and chapatis. In the morning, I would pick over the dal, wash it and put it in water to soak, if it needs soaking. I would also make the dough for the chapattis in advance, which will keep up to three or four days refrigerated.

About an hour before I want to serve dinner, I will start cooking the dal. While it is simmering, I will prepare the vegetables and make the raita. Finally, I will cook the chapatis. They will take about six to eight minutes to cook, once the griddle is heated. (If you do not wish to make your own chapatis, you may substitute frozen ones or even use pita.) Dals can be cooked ahead of time and heated just before serving. Make the baghar at the last minute to give the dal a fresh look. Most dals can be adapted to make excellent soups.

If you plan to cook a dal that takes longer to cook, for example, kidney beans, chickpeas or whole urd dal, you may prefer to use a crock pot. Put the dal in the crock pot in the morning and it will be ready for the evening meal.

Please refer to the separate chapters on breads, rice, desserts, appetizers and chutney, pickles and salads for brief explanations of how these categories fit into Indian meals.

Menu 1
[Serves 6 to 8 persons]

Sabut Masar (Whole Brown Lentils or Flageolets)

Gajjar Bhaji (Dry-cooked Carrots)

Bhindi Bhaji (Dry-cooked Okra)

Plain Rice

Chapatis

This menu is simple but delicious. The choice of vegetables is flexible: you may cook one or the other or both. The starch is equally flexible. You may wish to serve rice or chapatis, depending on your motivation and the time available. A menu can work with one dal, one vegetable and one starch. This is a simple menu, which a beginner may try and achieve good results.

I will tell you in some detail how I would prepare this meal to give you an idea of how to organize your time efficiently.

About an hour before I want to serve dinner, I will start cooking the dal. Make dough for chapatis. While it is simmering, I will prepare the vegetables and make the raita. Finally, I will make the chapatis. They will take about six to eight minutes to cook, once the griddle is heated. (If you are too busy to make your own chapatis, you may substitute frozen ones or even use pita.)

1

Sabut Masar
(Whole Brown Lentils or Flageolets)

1½ cups brown lentils or flageolets
2 to 4 whole cloves garlic, peeled
1 teaspoon ground ginger
1 teaspoons salt
¼ teaspoon turmeric
6 cups cold water
3 tablespoons vegetable oil
½ teaspoon cumin seeds
1 teaspoon black mustard seeds
½ teaspoon fennel seeds
1 medium onion, finely chopped
2 medium tomatoes, finely chopped
½ teaspoon cayenne pepper
1 teaspoon garam masala

Pick over the lentils and wash them under running water in a colander.

In a heavy 4-quart saucepan, combine the lentils with the garlic, ginger, salt, turmeric and water. Raise the heat to high and bring to a full boil. Lower the heat and simmer for about 30-40 minutes, stirring occasionally. Lentils and water should become smooth in consistency.

While the dal is cooking, prepare the baghar. Heat the oil in a small saucepan or skillet. Stir in the cumin, mustard and fennel seeds and cook until they sizzle and begin to darken. Add the onion and sauté until golden brown. Add the tomatoes, and cayenne and cook on medium, stirring frequently to prevent sticking or burning. Cook until the oil separates and the tomatoes are soft and dark and rich in color.

Pour the baghar into the dal and stir to blend. Simmer for 5 to 7 minutes. Adjust for salt. If the dal is too thick, add a little hot water. Sprinkle with garam masala and serve.

Gajjar Bhaji
(Dry-cooked Carrots)

2 pounds carrots
3 to 4 tablespoons oil
½ teaspoon mustard seeds
1 teaspoon cumin seeds
1 inch piece of fresh ginger, finely chopped
½ teaspoon turmeric
½ teaspoon cayenne pepper (optional)
1 teaspoon ground coriander
1 teaspoon ground cumin
1 teaspoon salt or to taste
1 teaspoon sugar

1 teaspoon amchur powder
or 1 tablespoon lemon juice
or 1 cup chopped tomatoes

¾ teaspoon garam masala
2 tablespoons cilantro finely chopped

Peel the carrots and slice them into thin rounds (slightly thinner than ¼ inch).

Heat the oil on medium in a deep skillet. Add the mustard seeds and cumin seeds. The cumin should sizzle and darken almost immediately. Stir in the ginger and brown it slightly.

Reduce the heat to medium low. Stir in the turmeric, cayenne, ground coriander and ground cumin. Mix well. Stir in the carrots and salt. Cover and cook for about 7 to 8 minutes or until the carrots are tender.

Add the sugar and amchur powder (or lemon juice or tomatoes). Raise the heat to high and cook until all the moisture is absorbed.

Sprinkle with the garam masala and chopped cilantro before serving.

Bhindi Bhaji
(Dry-cooked Okra)

1 pound okra
½ teaspoon turmeric
1 teaspoon ground coriander
1 teaspoon ground cumin
¾ teaspoon salt
4 tablespoons oil
½ teaspoon cumin seeds
1 cup chopped onion
1 to 2 green chili, finely chopped
2 teaspoons lime or lemon juice
¾ teaspoon garam masala

Wash the okra and dry it with a towel. Slice it into ½ inch rounds. Mix the turmeric, ground coriander, ground cumin and salt and sprinkle the mixture over the okra, stirring so that the okra is thoroughly covered.

Heat the oil on medium in a heavy skillet. When the oil is hot, add the cumin seeds, onion and chili. Sauté for a minute and then add the okra, mixing well. Cook covered, for about five minutes.

Stir in the lime or lemon juice and sauté uncovered on medium low for five to seven minutes. The lemon juice reduces the slimy texture of the okra and adds to the taste as well. Cook until the okra is tender but slightly firm.

Menu 2
[Serves 6 to 8 persons]

Masoor Dal with Vegetables

Panch Pooran Alu (Potatoes with Panch Pooran)

Plain Rice

I like to eat sambar, which is a soupy kind of South Indian dal eaten almost every day in that part of the country. This recipe is my version of a South Indian sambar dish. Traditionally it is quite spicy. I experimented and tried to make this dish more nutritious, more filling and a little less spicy. The dal can be made in advance and refrigerated; it tastes even better the second day. Most of the seasonings in this dish are readily available.

Since this dal takes a lot of time, the potato dish is quick and delicious and complements the dal.

Masoor Dal aur Sabzi
(Masoor Dal with Vegetables)

Sambar Powder:
- **4 dry red whole chilies**
- **4 tablespoons washed urd dal**
- **4 tablespoons grated unsweetened coconut**
- **2 tablespoons fenugreek seeds**
- **2 tablespoons coriander seeds**
- **2 tablespoons cumin seeds**

   Dry roast the ingredients for Sambar Powder. Cool and grind finely.

- **1 tablespoon vegetable oil**
- **1½ cups pink masoor dal, picked clean, washed and soaked for 30 minutes**
- **1 teaspoon cumin seeds**
- **1 teaspoon turmeric**
- **1½ teaspoons salt**
- **7 cups of water**
- **1 medium onion coarsely chopped**
- **12—15 pearl onions, peeled and halved**
- **1 small or ½ large eggplant sliced in thin 2" long slices**
- **2 small zucchinis, sliced the same size as eggplant**
- **½ cup green beans, cut in 1 inch pieces**
- **3 medium tomatoes, chopped**
- **1 or 2 jalapeño chilis, diced**

   (You should have 4 to 6 cups of vegetables.)

- **3 tablespoons oil**
- **1 teaspoon black mustard seeds**
- **2—4 whole cloves of garlic, peeled and minced**
- **1 tablespoon finely chopped fresh ginger**
- **¼ teaspoon turmeric**
- **1 teaspoon salt**
- **½ cup tamarind extract [pulp: page xix]**
- **or 3 tablespoons fresh lemon juice**
- **3 tablespoons sambar powder**

Drain the dal in a colander or large sieve.

Heat a large, heavy pot on medium. Add the oil and heat it to nearly smoking. Add cumin seeds; after they sizzle and darken, add dal, turmeric and salt. Stir to blend.

Add water. Cover and bring to a boil. Turn heat to low and simmer 20 minutes.

In a heavy 4 quart pot, heat 3 tablespoons oil on medium high. When the oil is near smoking, add the mustard seeds. Cover the pot and let the mustard seeds finish popping; add garlic and ginger. Reduce the heat to medium and sauté for 30 seconds to 1 minute.

Add the chopped onions and pearl onions and cook until transparent.

Add turmeric, salt, eggplant, green beans and zucchini. Stir to blend all ingredients. Cover and turn heat to low and cook for 5 minutes.

Add tomatoes and jalapeno chilis. Cook, covered, for 3 minutes.

Stir the cooked vegetables into the dal. Add the tamarind and sambar powder. Taste for salt and tartness. Adjust seasonings if necessary.

Simmer for another hour, stirring occasionally.

If you wish to serve the dal later, cool and refrigerate. Reheat on low heat. The flavor improves with keeping.

Note: *Other vegetables can be substituted, such as green bell peppers, okra, carrots or cauliflower.*

Panch Pooran Alu
(Potatoes with Panch Pooran)

1 pound potatoes
3 tablespoons oil
1 teaspoon panch pooran
2 dry red chilies
1 teaspoon sesame seeds
¼ teaspoon turmeric
1 teaspoon salt
1 green chili, finely chopped
3 tablespoons sour yogurt (If yogurt is not sour, add ½ teaspoon lemon juice.)

Boil the potatoes and cool them completely. Peel them and cut them into 3/4 inch cubes.

Heat the oil in a heavy skillet on medium. Add the panch pooran and the red chilies.

Remove the pan from the heat and add the sesame seeds. They should quickly take on a pinkish color. Add turmeric, salt, potatoes and chili. Return the skillet to the heat and mix the potatoes with the spices. Add 1 tablespoon yogurt, stir and cook for a couple of minutes until the moisture evaporates. Repeat with the rest of the yogurt, adding 1 tablespoon at a time. The potatoes should be a little crunchy and nicely coated with the spices.

Note: *If you boil the potatoes and refrigerate them for a few hours before peeling and chopping them, you will get better results.*

Menu 3
[Serves 6 to 8 persons]

Dhuli Moong Dal (Washed Moong Dal)

Alu Baigan Bhaji (Potatoes and Eggplant)

Raita with Cucumbers and Tomatoes

Chapatis

This menu is one of the most basic. Washed Moong Dal takes about 30 minutes to cook, and Potatoes and Eggplant can be prepared while the dal is cooking. This dal is easy on the stomach. In our family, when this dal is served, someone will ask jokingly, "Is somebody sick?" But I always enjoy this dal.

Dhuli Moong Dal
(Washed Moong Dal)

1½ cups washed moong dal
1 teaspoon oil
Small pinch asafoetida (optional)
½ teaspoon cumin seeds
½ teaspoon cayenne
½ teaspoon turmeric
1 teaspoon salt
4½ cups water

Clean the dal, removing small stones or bad pieces of dal. Soak the dal in 4 to 5 cups of water for 2 to 6 hours. Wash and rinse the dal in cold water and drain it.

In a three to four quart saucepan with a heavy bottom, heat the oil on medium high. Add the asafoetida and cumin seeds. As soon as the cumin begins to sizzle, add the cayenne, turmeric and drained dal. Cook the mixture, stirring frequently, for three to four minutes so that the dal is coated with the oil and spices.

Add the salt and water. Bring to the boil. Reduce the heat to medium low. Cook, covered, stirring occasionally. After 10 to 15 minutes, the dal will be tender, but the water will still be separate. After another 10 to 15 minutes, the dal will become creamy and thick; the consistency will be like a cream soup.

For baghar:
1½ tablespoons oil or ghee
½ teaspoon cumin seeds
¼ cup finely chopped onion
1 medium tomato, finely chopped
½ teaspoon paprika
½ teaspoon garam masala
2 teaspoons finely chopped cilantro

In a small skillet, heat the oil or ghee on medium. Add cumin seeds. When they begin to sizzle, add the chopped onion and cook until golden. Add the tomatoes and cook until they are soft and the oil begins to separate. Add paprika and garam masala. Stir into the dal and garnish with chopped cilantro before serving.

Alu Baigan Bhaji
(Eggplant and Potatoes)

1 teaspoon cumin seeds
1 teaspoon coriander seeds
1½ pounds oriental eggplant
1 pound new or red potatoes
4 to 5 tablespoons vegetable oil
1 teaspoon black mustard seeds
1 teaspoon cumin seeds
1 large onion, sliced
½ teaspoon turmeric
½ to 1 teaspoon cayenne
1 teaspoon salt
2-3 teaspoons amchur or 2 to3 teaspoons fresh lemon juice

Dry roast and grind the cumin and coriander seeds.

Wash the eggplants and cut them lengthwise into 2 inch slices. Cut each lengthwise slice crosswise. You should have pieces that are 2 inches long and about 3/4 inch thick. Peel the potatoes and slice them 1/2 inch thick like french fries.

Heat the oil on medium high in a heavy bottomed skillet. Add the mustard and cumin seeds. As soon as they start sizzling, add the onion. Sauté the onion until it is golden. Add the turmeric, cayenne and potatoes. Cook, stirring frequently, for about five minutes. The spices should coat the potatoes.

Stir in the eggplant and salt. Reduce the heat to medium low and cook, covered, for about 5 to 7 minutes, stirring occasionally. If the vegetables begin to stick to the bottom of the skillet, add a little water. Continue cooking until the vegetables are tender.

Stir in the amchur or lemon juice. Sprinkle with dry roasted cumin and coriander seeds and serve.

Menu 4
[Serves 6 to 8 persons]

Tariwale Alu Mattar (Pea and Tomato Curry)

Band Gobi, Saunf Aur Til Ke Sath (Cabbage with Fennel and Sesame Seeds)

Raita with Zucchini

Chapatis

Peas and cabbage used to be seasonal vegetables. Now, even in India, they are available year round, but they taste better in the winter. Here you can cook them year round. When I was growing up, it used to be a treat to eat peas, but to get the treat, we had to shell the peas, which was a chore. This is a simple, basic form of curry. The cabbage provides a totally different flavor, which complements the curry.

Tariwale Alu Matar
(Curried Peas and Potatoes)

4 tablespoons oil
¹/³ cup finely chopped onion
1 tablespoon finely minced fresh ginger
¼ teaspoon turmeric
½ teaspoon cayenne pepper
½ teaspoon paprika
1 teaspoon ground cumin
1 teaspoon ground coriander
1 cup tomatoes, skinned if desired and chopped
3 to 4 medium potatoes, peeled and cut into 1½ inch cubes
3 cups peas, fresh or frozen
2 cups water
½ cup yogurt
½ teaspoon garam masala
½ cup cilantro, chopped

In a heavy three-quart saucepan, heat the oil on medium. Add onion and ginger and cook, covered, for a minute or two. Uncover and sauté until the onions and ginger turn golden and the oil begins to separate. Stir in the turmeric, cayenne, paprika, cumin, coriander and tomatoes.

Cook, stirring occasionally, until the oil begins to separate again. Add the potatoes and sauté. If you are using fresh peas, add them at this point. Cook the potatoes in the sauce for about 5 minutes and then add the frozen peas. Add water. When the curry begins to cook vigorously, reduce the heat to low and cook until the potatoes are tender.

Beat the yogurt until smooth and stir into the curry. Cook for another few minutes, until the oil rises to the top.

Stir in the garam masala and half the chopped cilantro. Garnish with the remaining cilantro.

Bund Gobi, Saunf Aur Til Ke Sath
(Cabbage with Fennel and Sesame Seeds)

1 large head of cabbage (about 1½ pounds)
2 medium onions
1 large red bell pepper
3-4 tablespoons peanut oil or vegetable oil
2-3 dry red chilies
1 teaspoon whole cumin seeds
1 teaspoon whole fennel seeds
2 tablespoons sesame seeds
1 teaspoon salt or to taste

Remove the hard outside layer of cabbage leaves and cut the remaining into quarters. Cut away the core. Cut the cabbage into fine shreds. Cut the onions in half lengthwise and then cut the halves crosswise to make half rings. Cut the red pepper into long, thin slices.

Heat the oil in a wok or large, heavy skillet on medium. Add the chilies, cumin, fennel and sesame seeds and stir for a few seconds. Add the onions and sauté, stirring occasionally, until they begin to turn light golden brown. Add the cabbage and salt and mix them into the spices and onions by stirring with two spatulas. Cover and cook on medium low for 2-3 minutes. Add the red pepper slices; stir and cook uncovered on medium heat for 4-5 minutes until the moisture has evaporated.

Menu 5
[Serve 6 to 8 persons]

Masoor Dal (Pink Lentils with Tomatoes)

Green Beans with Mustard Seeds and Ginger

Bharta (Pureed Eggplant with Onions and Tomatoes)

Plain Rice or Parathas

Pink masoor dal is widely available and takes less time to prepare than any other dal. It is light and delicious and can be served for lunch or dinner with rice or bread. Green beans and eggplant are a wonderful complement to the dish, but if you are in a hurry you can make do with one or the other vegetable.

Bharta is a kind of delicacy, which is loved by many people (except my husband, who dislikes eggplant in almost any form). It also works very well when served as a spread on bread or pita for an appetizer.

Masoor Dal aur Tomatoes
(Pink Lentils with Tomatoes)

2 cups pink masoor dal, picked over and soaked in cold water for 20 to 30 minutes
1 tablespoon vegetable oil
1 teaspoon whole cumin seeds
½ teaspoon turmeric
1 teaspoon cayenne
6 cups water
1 teaspoon salt
3 to 4 tablespoons vegetable oil, butter or ghee
1 medium onion, finely chopped
2 medium tomatoes, chopped
1 teaspoon garam masala
Chopped cilantro

Drain the dal in a colander and rinse it by letting cold water run over it.

In a heavy 4-quart saucepan, heat the oil on medium high to nearly smoking. Add the cumin seeds. They should sizzle and darken almost immediately. Remove the pot from the burner and add the turmeric, cayenne and dal. Return the pot to the burner and stir to blend.

Add the water and salt. Bring to a full boil. Stir and reduce the heat to low. Cover and let it simmer for 25 to 30 minutes.

For baghar:

In a small skillet, heat the oil, butter or ghee. Add the onions and cook on medium until golden brown. Add the chopped tomatoes and cook, stirring frequently, until the tomatoes are cooked and the oil separates. Add 1 to 2 tablespoons of water if the mixture begins to burn or stick to the bottom of the pan.

Stir the baghar into the dal. Sprinkle with garam masala and garnish with cilantro.

Haree Phali Rai aur Adarak
(Green Beans with Mustard and Ginger)

1 pound fresh green beans
2 tablespoons oil
¼ teaspoon mustard seeds
1 tablespoon minced ginger
1 or 2 green chilies, finely chopped
¼ teaspoon ground turmeric
½ teaspoon ground cumin
½ teaspoon ground coriander
¾ teaspoon salt
1 tablespoon lemon juice
½ teaspoon garam masala

Trim and wash the beans and cut into 1/2" pieces.

Heat the oil on medium in a heavy 3 quart saucepan or skillet. Add the mustard seeds. As soon as they begin to sizzle, add the chopped ginger and green chilies. Sauté for a minute or so and add the turmeric, cumin, coriander, salt and green beans. Mix well, cover and cook on medium low for about 10 minutes. The beans should cook in their own juices. If the heat is low and the pot is heavy, you will not need to add water.

When the beans are barely tender but crisp, uncover the pot. Turn up the heat for a minute to evaporate any excess moisture. Add lemon juice and garam masala and heat it through.

Bharta
(Pureed Eggplant with Onions and Tomatoes)

2 medium eggplants
6 tablespoons oil
2 cups sliced onions
2 cups finely chopped tomatoes
2 green chilies, finely chopped
2 teaspoons ground coriander
1 teaspoon ground cumin
1 teaspoon paprika
1 teaspoon salt
½ cup cilantro, finely chopped
2 tablespoons yogurt

Wash and dry the eggplant. Make a few slits in the eggplant with a knife. Roast the eggplant on a grill or under a broiler or on a cake rack over a stove burner. Turn it carefully to char the skin. Let it cool and peel off the charred skin. Mash the eggplant.

Heat a skillet on medium. Add the oil and onions and cook, covered, for 3 to 4 minutes. Remove the cover and continue to cook, stirring occasionally, until the onions are golden brown on the edges. Add the tomatoes and chilies and continue cooking, stirring occasionally, until the oil begins to separate and the tomatoes are cooked. Mash the mixture with the back of a spatula.

Stir in the coriander, cumin, paprika and salt and half the cilantro. Mix well. Stir in the mashed eggplant. Cook the mixture on medium low to evaporate some of the moisture. The consistency of the mixture should have the consistency of mashed potatoes. Add the yogurt and cook 2 to 3 minutes.

Garnish with remaining cilantro.

Menu 6
[Serves 6 to 8 persons]

Washed Urd and Chana Dal

Alu Methi Bhaji (Potatoes with Fenugreek or Dill)

Band Gobi and Matar Bhaji (Cabbage and Peas)

Tomato Raita

Naan

Urd and chana dal is a most popular dal from Punjab and is widely used all over North India. This dal is an acquired taste, but I think you will find this version delicious and easy to fix. The combination of the two vegetables really complements this dal. Rice usually is not eaten with this dal, so serve it with naan instead.

Dhuli Urd Chana Dal Payaz aur Tamatar
(Washed Urd and Chana Dal with Onions and Tomatoes)

1½ cups washed urd dal
4 tablespoons chana dal
1 teaspoon oil
½ teaspoon cumin seeds
1 tablespoon finely chopped fresh ginger
¾ teaspoon cayenne
½ teaspoon turmeric
¾ to 1 teaspoon salt
4½ cups water

For baghar:
3 tablespoons oil or ghee
¼ cup chopped onions
½ cup chopped tomatoes
½ teaspoon paprika
½ teaspoon garam masala
2 tablespoons chopped cilantro

Pick over the dal and soak it for 2-3 hours.

Heat a 4 quart heavy bottomed saucepan on medium high. Heat 1 teaspoon oil. Add the cumin seeds. As soon as they begin to sizzle, add the chopped ginger. Stir and cook for a few seconds, and then add cayenne, turmeric and dal. Sauté for 2 to 3 minutes. Add salt and water and bring to a vigorous boil. Reduce the heat to medium low, cover the pot and cook for 30 to 40 minutes, stirring occasionally. The dal will be tender, but the water will be separate. Continue cooking until the mixture becomes thick and smooth.

Heat the oil or ghee in a small skillet. Add the chopped onions and sauté until they become golden in color. Add the chopped tomatoes and paprika and sauté until the tomatoes are cooked and the oil begins to separate. Add the garam masala. Mix the baghar gently into the dal. Garnish with cilantro before serving.

Alu Methi Bhaji
(Potatoes with Fenugreek or Dill)

3-4 tablespoons mustard oil, vegetable oil or a mixture of the two oils

1 teaspoon cumin seeds

2 dry red chilies

1 pound small new potatoes (red or white), unpeeled, washed, and cut into 1/2 to 3/4 inch pieces

½ cup dry fenugreek leaves soaked in 1/2 cup warm water *or*

2 cups fresh fenugreek leaves, washed and finely chopped *or*

1 cup fresh dill

¾ to 1 teaspoon salt

1 green chili, finely chopped

Heat oil on medium high in a heavy skillet. When the oil is very hot, add the cumin seeds, red chilies and potatoes. Stir to coat the potatoes with the oil. Cover and reduce the heat to medium. Cook the potatoes for about 5 minutes.

Add the fenugreek or dill, salt and green chilies. Reduce the heat to low and cook, covered, for another 5-7 minutes. When the potatoes are almost tender, remove the cover and gently sauté so that the potatoes are a little crispy.

Band Gobi and Matar Bhaji
(Cabbage and Peas)

1 pound cabbage
1 tablespoon fresh ginger
4 tablespoons oil
½ teaspoon black mustard seeds
½ teaspoon cumin seeds
½ teaspoon turmeric
½ teaspoon cayenne pepper
1 teaspoon ground cumin
1 teaspoon ground coriander
1 teaspoon salt
8 ounces frozen peas
1 teaspoon garam masala

Core the cabbage and slice it thin. Finely chop the ginger.

Heat the oil in a large skillet until it begins to smoke. Reduce the heat to medium and add the mustard seeds; when they start to sizzle, add the cumin seeds, turmeric and cayenne. Stir in the cabbage, chopped ginger, ground cumin, coriander and salt. Mix well and cover the skillet. Raise the heat to high. Steam the cabbage for about 5 minutes; add peas and mix well. Cover the skillet and cook for another 5 minutes.

Uncover the skillet and cook on high until all the moisture evaporates from the skillet. Turn the heat down and sauté for about 5—7 minutes. Sprinkle with garam masala just before serving.

Menu 7
[Serves 6 to 8 persons]

Khati Arhar Dal (Sour Pigeon Peas)

Alu Matar Bhaji (Potatoes and Peas)

Karam Saag Bhaji (Dry-cooked Kohlrabi)

Plain Rice and/or Dill Paratha

This dal is very popular in Northern India. In many families, it is cooked almost every day, accompanied by changing vegetables. In Punjab it is less popular, but still enjoyed by many families, including my own. This dal goes very well with rice together with chapatis.

Khati Arhar Dal
(Sour Pigeon Peas)

1½ cups arhar dal (pigeon peas)
1 tablespoon oil
½ teaspoon crushed red pepper
½ teaspoon turmeric
1 teaspoon salt
4½ cups water
2-3 tablespoons tamarind pulp[page xix] or lemon juice

For Baghar:
2 tablespoons ghee or oil
Small pinch asafoetida (optional)
1 teaspoon cumin seed
½ teaspoon cayenne or paprika
½ teaspoon garam masala

Pick over the dal. Soak it for at least 2 hours, up to 4-6 hours. Wash well and drain. Heat oil in a 3-4 quart saucepan on medium. Add red pepper, turmeric and drained dal. Stir and cook the dal for 3-4 minutes. Add salt and water. Bring to the boil. Reduce the heat to medium low, cover and cook for 30 minutes. The dal should be tender, but it may not be creamy. Let it simmer for another 10-15 minutes, until the dal is creamy. Stir in the tamarind pulp or lemon juice and simmer for another 5 minutes.

For the baghar, heat the ghee or oil in a small skillet. Add the asafoetida, cumin seeds, cayenne or paprika and garam masala. Pour over the dal and gently stir to blend.

Alu Matar Bhaji
(Potatoes and Peas)

3 tablespoons oil
¼ teaspoon black mustard seeds
½ teaspoon cumin seeds
1½ tablespoons minced ginger root
¼ to ½ teaspoon cayenne
½ teaspoon turmeric
¾ teaspoon ground cumin
1 teaspoon ground coriander
¾ to1 teaspoon salt
2 cups new red or white potatoes, peeled and cut into ¾ inch cubes
2 cups fresh or frozen peas
½ teaspoon garam masala
2 tablespoons chopped cilantro

Heat the oil on medium. Add the mustard seeds. As soon as they start to sizzle, add the cumin seeds. Stir and add the ginger. Sauté for 30 seconds and add cayenne, turmeric, ground cumin and coriander. If you are using fresh peas, add peas and potatoes and sauté for about 5 minutes. If you are using frozen peas, sauté potatoes for about 5 minutes; then add peas and sauté for 2 more minutes. Add salt.

Cover the pot and reduce the heat to medium low. Cook for another 5-7 minutes or until the potatoes are tender. Stir in the garam masala and cilantro.

Karam Saag Bhaji
(Dry-cooked Kohlrabi)

4-5 kohlrabies with their greens (about 3 cups bulbs and 2 cups greens)
3 tablespoons mustard or canola oil
1-2 dry red chilies
Small pinch asafoetida (optional)
1 teaspoon fennel seeds
1 green chili, finely chopped
¾ to1 teaspoon salt

Peel the kohlrabi and cut it into pieces that are shaped like French fries. Finely chop the tender greens.

Heat the oil on medium high. Add the red chilies, asafoetida, fennel seeds, kohlrabi and greens, green chili and salt. Stir to coat the kohlrabi with the oil and spices. Cover the pan. Reduce the heat to medium low. Stir from time to time to ensure that the kohlrabi is not sticking to the bottom of the pan.

In about 10 minutes, it should be tender but still retain some moisture. Uncover the pan and sauté for another 5 minutes. If kohlrabi is not very tender it may take a little longer to be cooked. You may have to add a little bit of water.

Menu 8
[Serves 6 to 8 persons]

Whole Moong Dal

Dahi Bhindi Bhaji (Okra Cooked in Yogurt)

Khumbi Matar (Pea and Mushroom Curry)

Plain Rice and/or Chapatis

Plain Yogurt

This dal takes longer to cook than the dals that have appeared in previous menus. You can achieve the best results if it is simmered on low heat. In the Western kitchen, slow cookers work best. If you don't have time for a slow cooker, you can cook the dal in a pressure cooker or on the stove. When the dal is cooked until it is smooth and creamy and has the consistency of a thick soup, it is delicious served with rice.

Whole Moong Dal

1½ cups whole moong dal
½ teaspoon crushed red chilies
1 teaspoon salt
½ teaspoon turmeric
½ teaspoon ground ginger
7 cups water
2 tablespoons ghee or butter
1 small onion, finely chopped
1 large tomato
½ teaspoon cayenne or paprika

Pick over the dal and wash thoroughly. Put the dal into a crock- pot or heavy saucepan with the chilies, salt, turmeric, ginger and water. Cook for 7 to 8 hours in the crock-pot. If you are cooking the dal on the stove, bring to the boil, reduce the heat to medium and cook for an hour or so. The dal should split and become tender, but the liquid will still be separate from the beans. Reduce the heat to medium low and cook for another 45 minutes to an hour or until the dal has become creamy.

For the baghar

Heat the butter or ghee and sauté the onions until they are golden. Add the tomato, cover the pan and cook for 2-3 minutes. Uncover and stir constantly until the tomato is cooked and the ghee starts to separate. Add the paprika or cayenne. Gently stir the baghar into the dal.

Dahi Bhindi Bhaji
(Okra Cooked in Yogurt)

3 cups tender okra, about 1½ pound (The okra should not xceed
2-2½ inches in length.)
1 cup oil for deep frying
1 tablespoon oil
1 teaspoon cumin seeds
1 teaspoon poppy seeds
½ teaspoon cayenne pepper
½ to ¾ teaspoon salt
¾ cup sour yogurt

Wash the okra and pat it dry. Remove stems. Heat 1 cup oil in a small wok or skillet and fry the okra until it turns a little pink and crisp. Drain on a paper towel.

Heat 1 tablespoon oil in a skillet on medium. (You can use the same oil you used to fry the okra.) Add the cumin seeds, poppy seeds, cayenne, salt and yogurt. Cook for a few minutes, stirring, until the liquid begins to evaporate. Stir in the fried okra and let it simmer for 2-3 minutes.

Khumbi Matar
(Pea and Mushroom Curry)

4 to 5 tablespoons oil
1 large onion, finely chopped
1½ inch piece of ginger, scraped and minced
2 to 3 cloves garlic, minced
2 large ripe tomatoes, chopped (peeled if desired)
½ teaspoon turmeric
1 teaspoon ground cumin
1 teaspoon ground coriander
½ teaspoon cayenne pepper
½ teaspoon paprika
¾ to 1 teaspoon salt
12 ounces button mushrooms, wiped and halved
1 pound frozen peas
½ cup water
½ cup yogurt
½ cup chopped cilantro
1 teaspoon garam masala

Heat the oil in a heavy saucepan on medium high. Add the onion, ginger and garlic and sauté until the mixture is a golden color and the oil begins to separate.

Reduce the heat to medium. Add the tomatoes and cook until the oil begins to separate again.

Stir in the turmeric, cumin, coriander, cayenne, paprika and salt. Add the mushrooms and cook them in the sauce for about 5 minutes. Stir in the peas and water. Bring to the boil and cook for about 5 minutes.

Beat the yogurt smooth and add to the curry. Simmer for 5 minutes. Sprinkle on the chopped cilantro and garam masala and serve.

Menu 9
[Serves 6 to 8 persons]

Palak Panir (Spinach with Panir)

Chana Dal Sukhi (Dry Chana Dal)

Tamatar Pulao (Rice with Tomatoes)

Alu Raita (Potato Raita)

Onion Naan

This is a wonderful menu. If you master the technique of making panir, palak panir is not a time-consuming dish. "Saag" is a generic name for greens, which might be mustard greens, Swiss chard, turnip greens or spinach. Once you are comfortable with the recipe, it is fun to experiment with different combinations of greens. This menu is a good company meal, but it can be used for an everyday meal as well.

Palak Panir
(Spinach with Panir)

¼ cup water
3 10—ounce packages of frozen chopped spinach
1 10—ounce package of frozen chopped broccoli
1 large onion, coarsely chopped
2 large tomatoes, chopped
1 or 2 jalapeño chilis, finely chopped
4 cloves of whole garlic, peeled
2 tablespoons fresh ginger, finely chopped
1 to 1½ teaspoons salt or to taste
½ cup sour cream
Panir made from 1 gallon milk, cut into cubes and fried
according to instructions [see pp xxi-xxii]
4 tablespoons butter 1 teaspoon paprika
Tomato or red pepper slices for garnish

Bring a pot of water to the boil. Remove from heat and soak the panir cubes for 30 minutes.

In a large, heavy pot or deep skillet, combine water, frozen vegetables, onion, tomatoes, jalapeño, garlic and ginger. Turn heat to low. Let the vegetables thaw and cook with the other ingredients for an hour, covered. Remove the cover and raise the heat to medium high to evaporate as much excess liquid as possible without burning the mixture. Stir continuously for a couple of minutes. Turn off the heat.

Puree the mixture in a Cuisinart or with a hand-held blender, in more than one batch if necessary. Return to the large pot and add salt. Drain the panir and gently stir the panir cubes into the pureed spinach. Stir and simmer gently on low heat for 1/2 hour, stirring occasionally. Add sour cream; stir and heat through. Keep the cover on, as there will be some spattering.

Melt 4 tablespoons butter in a small skillet on low heat. Add paprika. Pour over the saag panir. Garnish with thin slices of tomatoes and/or red pepper.

Note: *This dish can be made ahead and reheated just before serving. Unfried panir may be substituted for the fried panir cubes.*

Chana Dal Sukhi
(Dry Chana Dal)

2 cups chana dal, soaked in 4 cups water for at least two hrs.
1 tablespoon vegetable oil
½ teaspoon black mustard seeds
1 teaspoon whole cumin seeds
2 inch piece of fresh ginger, peeled and finely chopped
½ teaspoon turmeric
½ teaspoon salt
½ teaspoon cayenne pepper (optional)
2½ cups water
1½ teaspoons lemon juice

For the baghar:
    2 tablespoons butter
    1 medium onion, chopped
    ½ teaspoon sweet paprika
    1 teaspoon garam masala
    Chopped cilantro for garnish

Wash and drain the dal.

In a heavy pot, heat the oil on medium heat and add the mustard seeds and cumin. Cover the pot until the mustard seeds stop popping. Sauté the chopped ginger for a minute. Add the dal, turmeric, salt and cayenne pepper. Sauté for about 4 minutes on medium high.

Add the water and bring to a boil. Reduce the heat to medium low and simmer for 30 to 35 minutes, stirring occasionally. When the liquid is almost evaporated, and the dal is tender, turn off the heat and steam cook with the lid on until the moisture evaporates completely. Stir in the lemon juice.

For baghar

In a small skillet, melt the butter and sauté the onion until golden brown. Add paprika and garam masala. Pour the baghar into the dal and gently stir in. Garnish with chopped cilantro.

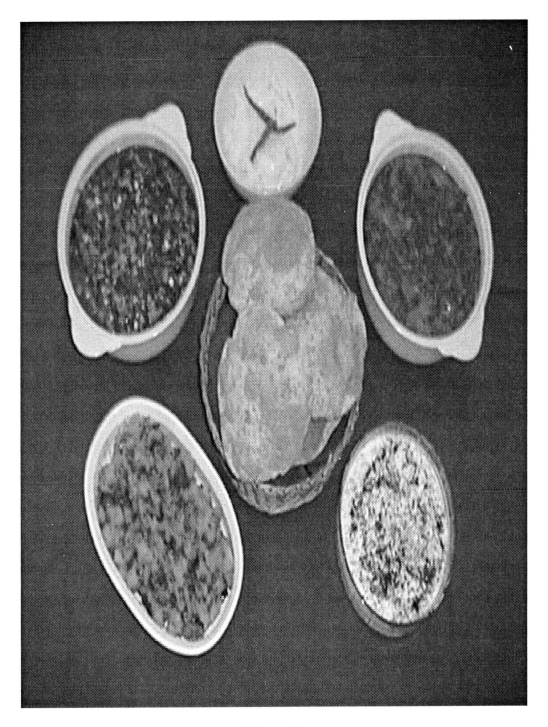

Menu 10

Menu 10
[Serves 8 to 10 persons]

Chana Masala (Chick Peas with Spicy Gravy)

Dahi Alu (Potatoes with Yogurt)

Kadoo Bhaji (Pumpkin Vegetable)

Boondi Raita

Poori

This menu is for a very traditional Indian festive meal and is cooked by many families for any religious holiday. As you may notice, this menu includes no onions or garlic, in the Ayurvedic tradition. Growing up, we loved this food, and my daughter still claims this is one of her favorite meals.

Chana Masala
(Chick Peas with Spicy Gravy)

2 cups chick peas
7 cups water
½ teaspoon baking soda
1 teaspoon oil
2 teaspoons salt
3 bay leaves
1 teaspoon ground ginger

Pick over the chick peas and wash them in two or three changes of water until the water is clear. Soak in 6 cups water and baking soda overnight. Pour into the pressure cooker with oil, salt, bay leaves and ginger. Turn heat to high. When pressure builds and steam starts to rise, reduce the heat to medium low and keep under pressure for 15 minutes. (If you are not using the pressure cooker, combine the ingredients in a 4- to 5-quart pot and bring to a quick boil. Turn the heat to medium and cook 30 to 45 minutes. You may have to add another cup of water). Chickpeas should be tender to the touch but still hold their shape.

1½ tablespoons coriander seeds
2 teaspoons cumin seeds
1 teaspoon peppercorns
10 cloves
2 1"-inch pieces stick cinnamon
1 teaspoon cardamom seeds
2 inch piece of fresh ginger coarsely chopped
½ cup cilantro coarsely chopped
2 hot green chilies
¼ cup tamarind pulp or 6 tablespoons lemon juice

In an iron skillet, dry roast the whole spices on medium heat, stirring constantly, until they turn dark brown. Cool and grind them in a coffee grinder.

In a blender, combine 2 tablespoons water with ginger, cilantro and chilies. Blend for 30 seconds. Add the roasted spices and blend for additional 15 seconds. Stir the mixture into the chick peas. Rinse the blender with 1/4 cup water and add to the chick pea mixture. Add the tamarind pulp or lemon juice. Reduce the heat to medium low and cook the chick peas, covered, for 20 to 25 minutes.

Note: *Do not add all the ground spices at once. Add according to your individual taste.*

For the baghar:
4 tablespoons oil
½ teaspoon paprika for garnish
2-3 hot green chilies
Chopped cilantro

Heat the oil for a few minutes in a skillet until it is medium hot. Turn off the heat and let the oil cool a little. Stir in the paprika. Pour the mixture over the chick peas and garnish with cilantro and chilies.

For the relish:
2 medium sweet or red onions, thinly sliced
Juice of one lemon or lime
½ teaspoon salt

Peel the onions and cut into thin slices. Soak them in iced water for one half hour.

Drain the onions and place them in bowl and add juice of one lemon or lime and salt. Mix and serve with chana.

Dahi Alu
(Potatoes with Yogurt)

10 medium-sized red or white potatoes
4 tablespoons oil
1 teaspoon whole cumin seeds
1½ inch piece fresh ginger, finely chopped
2 large tomatoes, blanched and chopped
1 teaspoon ground cumin
1 teaspoon ground coriander
1 teaspoon paprika
1 teaspoon turmeric
½ teaspoon cayenne pepper (optional)
1½ teaspoons salt or to taste
1 cup yogurt, beaten smooth
1¼ cups water
1 teaspoon garam masala
Cilantro for garnish

Boil potatoes in salted water until tender, about 15 to 20 minutes. When they are cool enough to handle, peel them and cut them into small cubes.

In a heavy, deep saucepan, heat the oil on medium high. When the oil is hot, add the cumin seeds. They should sizzle and turn dark as they rise to the surface. Add the chopped ginger and fry for a minute. Stir in the tomatoes and cook for 8 to 10 minutes, stirring often. When the tomatoes are cooked and the oil has separated, add the ground cumin, coriander, paprika, turmeric, cayenne and salt. Stir in the potatoes and yogurt and bring to the boil.

Add the water and return to the boil. Reduce the heat to medium low and simmer, covered, for about 15 minutes.

When ready to serve, stir in the garam masala and garnish with chopped cilantro.

Kadoo Bhaji
(Pumpkin Vegetable)

1½ teaspoons cumin seeds
2 tablespoons coriander seeds
6 tablespoons vegetable oil
3 teaspoons panch pooran
1 to 2 teaspoons salt
1 teaspoon turmeric
1 teaspoon paprika or cayenne pepper
8 cups pumpkin, peeled and cut into 1" cubes
1 tablespoon sugar
2 or 3 green chilies or jalapeños, very finely chopped
2 tablespoons amchur or juice of 1 to 2 limes

Dry roast and grind the cumin and coriander seeds. Set aside.

In a wide, heavy skillet, heat the oil on medium. Test the temperature of the oil by dropping in a few cumin seeds. If they sizzle, add all of the whole spices. Stir to mix the spices with oil and brown them for 5 to 10 seconds.

Add salt, turmeric, paprika and the pumpkin pieces, stirring well. The oil and spices should coat the pumpkin pieces. Cover and cook on medium low, for about 20 minutes or until the pumpkin is tender, stirring frequently to prevent burning.

Add sugar, jalapeños and amchur or lime juice. Taste and adjust seasoning. Add the roasted and ground cumin and coriander seeds and mix well. Serve hot.

Note: *Panch Pooram* recipe is in the chapter on spices [page xviii].

Menu 11
[Serves 6 to 8 persons]

Matar Panir (Pea and Panir Curry)

Alu Gobi (Cauliflower with Potatoes)

Asparagus with Coconut and Sesame Seeds

Cucumber Raita

Parathas

When I was growing up, this menu was always popular in the winter because of the availability of peas and cauliflower. But now we can make it year round. Matar panir is always considered a delicacy, and it is usually cooked on special occasions. As the directions for panir indicate, it is important to pour boiling water over the fried panir cubes and soak them for 30 minutes to an hour to obtain a very soft panir.

Asparagus was not included in traditional Indian cuisine. This recipe is the result of my experimentation with a food that was new to me.

41

Matar Panir
(Pea and Panir Curry)

Panir made from 1 gallon 2% milk, cut in cubes and fried according to instructions [pps: xxi-xxii]
1 large or two medium onions, coarsely chopped
2 inch piece fresh ginger, scraped and minced
1 or 2 jalapeño chilis, chopped (optional)
6 tablespoons of oil
1 tablespoon butter (optional)
½ teaspoon turmeric
1 teaspoon ground cumin
1 teaspoon ground coriander
1 teaspoon paprika
2 large or 3 medium tomatoes finely chopped
20 ounce package frozen peas
2 to 2½ cups of water
1½ teaspoons salt or to taste
½ cup yogurt
1 teaspoon garam masala
Cilantro for garnish, chopped

In a food processor or blender, grind together the onions, ginger and jalapeños.

In a large, heavy saucepan (preferably nonstick), heat the oil and butter on medium. Stir the ground onion mixture into the heated oil. Cook the mixture, stirring often, until it is golden in color and the oil separates. Add the turmeric, cumin, coriander and paprika. Mix well. Add the finely chopped tomatoes. Cover and cook, stirring frequently, until the tomatoes thicken; it may take 15 to 20 minutes. Add a couple of tablespoons of hot water if the mixture sticks to the bottom of the saucepan; stir and scrape to loosen. Cook until the oil separates from the tomatoes (about 10—15 minutes).

Stir in the peas and cook for 2 to 3 minutes. Add water and salt and bring to a boil. Reduce heat to low and simmer for 10 minutes. Add the panir cubes and yogurt and simmer on low heat for 10 to 15 minutes. The dish is ready to serve when the oil begins to float on top. When ready to serve, sprinkle on the garam masala and garnish with cilantro.

Note: *Unfried panir can be substituted for the fried panir cubes.*

Alu Gobi
(Cauliflower with Potatoes)

1 medium cauliflower
3 medium smooth-skinned red potatoes
5 to 6 tablespoons vegetable oil
1 teaspoon cumin seeds
2 tablespoons minced fresh ginger
½ teaspoon turmeric
1 teaspoon ground cumin
1 teaspoon ground coriander
¼ teaspoon cayenne pepper or to taste or 1 small green jalapeño, finely chopped, or both
1 teaspoon salt or to taste
1 teaspoon garam masala
Chopped fresh cilantro for garnish

Wash the cauliflower and cut into 1½ inch florets. Cut the potatoes into 1 inch cubes.

Heat a large, heavy skillet on medium and add the oil. Test the oil by dropping in one cumin seed; if it sizzles, the oil is ready. Add the cumin seeds and brown them for 2—3 seconds. Immediately add the ginger and sauté for 1 minute. Add the turmeric, ground cumin and coriander and cayenne pepper and/or jalapeño. Sauté for a couple of seconds.

Add the potatoes and stir them to mix and coat them with the oil and spices. Sauté them for a minute or so.

Stir in the cauliflower and salt; mix it well. Reduce the heat to medium low. Cover tightly. The salt should release the water from the cauliflower if it is fresh. If not, you can add 2—3 tablespoons water to prevent sticking or burning. Cook for about 10 minutes, gently stirring every 5 minutes or so. Add another tablespoon of water if necessary. Turn heat to medium low and cook until tender. The vegetables are ready when a knife pierces the cauliflower and potatoes easily. When no moisture is left, sprinkle garam masala over the top.

Garnish with chopped cilantro.

Asparagus with Coconut and Sesame Seeds

1½ pounds asparagus, cut into 1 to 1½ inch pieces
2 tablespoons unsweetened grated coconut
¼ cup chopped cilantro
1 green chili, finely chopped
2 tablespoons lime juice
1 teaspoon salt
4 tablespoons vegetable oil
1 teaspoon mustard seeds
2 whole red chilies
1 tablespoon sesame seeds
1 large red pepper, thinly sliced
½ teaspoon freshly ground black pepper

Steam the asparagus pieces briefly. They should retain some crunch.

In a small bowl, mix the coconut, cilantro, green chili, lime juice and salt and set aside.

Heat the oil in a large skillet on medium. Add the mustard seeds, red chilies and sesame seeds. As soon as they begin to sizzle, add the red pepper, steamed asparagus and coconut mixture. Cook for about 5 to 7 minutes. The asparagus should be tender but still crunchy. Sprinkle with freshly ground black pepper.

Menu 12
[Serves 8 to 10 persons]

Makhani Urd (Creamy Black Beans with Kidney Beans)

Khata Meetha Baigan (Sweet and Sour Eggplant)

Gobi Tamatar (Cauliflower with Tomatoes)

Sweet Onion and Mint Raita

Naan or Panir-stuffed Naan

Plain Rice

In Punjab, Makhani Urd is considered the king of dals. It is rich, creamy and delicious, and it can also be used as a hearty soup. The sweet and sour eggplant really complements the dal, with totally different spices. The simple dish of cauliflower that completes the menu is my family's favorite.

Makhani Urd
(Creamy Black Beans with Kidney Beans)

1½ cups small black Urd dal
½ cup red kidney beans
7 cups water
2 tablespoons minced fresh ginger
2 cloves garlic
1 to 1½ teaspoons crushed red pepper
4 bay leaves
2 cups whole or 2% milk
2 teaspoons salt

For baghar:
3 tablespoons oil and 1 tablespoon butter
1 cup finely chopped onions
2 cups chopped fresh or canned tomatoes
1 teaspoon garam masala
4 tablespoons sour cream
1 teaspoon paprika

Pick over the dal carefully. Wash it in several changes of water. Put the dal in a crock-pot and add the water, ginger, garlic, red pepper and bay leaves. Cook for about 4 hours in the crock-pot. (If you prefer to cook the dal on the stove, bring it to the boil. Reduce the heat to medium low and cook for about an hour.) The dal should be split and tender; the gravy will be watery.

Add the milk and salt and simmer on low for a couple of hours. The dal should be creamy and smooth and should have the consistency of a thick soup.

In a small skillet, heat the oil and butter on medium. Add the onions and sauté them until they are golden. Add the tomatoes and cook until the oil begins to separate. Pour the garam masala, sour cream and paprika over the dal and gently stir in.

This dish can be served as a hearty winter soup.

Khata-Meetha Baigan
(Sweet and Sour Eggplant)

2 pounds long Italian or oriental eggplant
1 tablespoon salt
1 tablespoon sesame seeds
1 tablespoon unsweetened grated coconut
2 dried hot red chilies
1½ teaspoons coriander seeds
2 teaspoons cumin seeds
6 tablespoons oil
1 teaspoon mustard seeds
2 medium onions, minced
2 to 3 cloves garlic, minced
1 teaspoon turmeric
5 tablespoons tamarind paste
5 tablespoons brown sugar

Wash the eggplant. Cut it into 2 inch slices and cut each slice in half or quarters. Put the eggplant pieces in a colander. Sprinkle them with the salt, mix well and let them stand for 30 minutes.

Dry roast the sesame seeds, coconut, chilies, coriander and cumin. Let the spices cool for a few minutes and then grind them in a coffee grinder.

Heat the oil in a heavy skillet. Add the mustard seeds. When they begin to sizzle, stir in the onion and garlic. Sauté on medium until they are golden. Stir in the turmeric, eggplant and ground roasted spices. Sprinkle the mixture with a little water. Cover the pan and cook for 5 to 7 minutes on medium. Add the tamarind and brown sugar and simmer for 15 to 20 minutes. The eggplant should be nicely glazed and tender.

Gobi Tamatar
(Cauliflower with Tomatoes)

½ cup yogurt
1½ tablespoons minced fresh ginger
½ teaspoon cayenne pepper or 1 teaspoon paprika
1 cup chopped tomato
2 tablespoons minced green onion
1 or 2 fresh green chilies, finely chopped
1 cup finely chopped cilantro
1 teaspoon salt
½ teaspoon turmeric
1 teaspoon ground cumin
1 teaspoon ground coriander
1 large-sized cauliflower
4 tablespoons oil
1 teaspoon garam masala

Mix the yogurt, ginger, tomato, onions, chilies, half the cilantro, salt and the remaining spices except the garam masala.

Wash the cauliflower and cut it into 1 to 1½ inch florets. Heat a heavy bottomed skillet on medium high and add oil and ensure that oil spreads evenly over the bottom of the pan. Add the cauliflower in a single layer and pour the yogurt mixture over it. Cover the pan tightly and cook for 5 to 7 minutes, shaking the pan occasionally.

Remove the lid and gently mix the cauliflower with the yogurt mixture. Turn up the heat to evaporate the moisture, taking care not to overcook the cauliflower. Sprinkle with garam masala and garnish with the remaining chopped cilantro.

Menu 13
[Serves 8 to 10 persons]

Shahi Panir (Panir with Bell Peppers)

Alu Palak Bhaji (Spinach and Potatoes)

Sukhi Moong Dal (Dry Moong Dal)

Mattar Pulao (Rice with Peas) and/or Methi Paratha

Boondi Raita (Raita with Small Gram Flour Dumplings)

This menu reflects my Jain background. Onions and garlic are not used in this cuisine, but once you try these dishes, you will not miss them. The menu is delicious and very appealing to the eye.

Shahi Panir
(Panir with Bell Peppers)

8-10 large tomatoes, coarsely chopped
2 green chilies, chopped
2 cups water
8 to 10 green cardamoms
3 to 4" cinnamon stick
3 bay leaves
½ teaspoon turmeric
1¼ teaspoons salt or to taste
Panir made from 1 gallon of milk, cut into 1" inch cubes but not fried
1 tablespoon dried fenugreek leaves
3 tablespoons butter
1 large green pepper, cut into ¾" chunks
½ red pepper, cut into ¾" pieces
1 teaspoon paprika
½ cup half-and-half or ¼ cup heavy cream
1 teaspoon garam masala

Tie the cardamom pods, cinnamon stick and bay leaves into a thin muslin cloth to form a pouch and place it, with the tomatoes, into a 4 quart saucepan. Cook the tomatoes and green chilies with 1 cup of water until the tomatoes are tender. Take the pouch of spices out and save it. Puree the mixture and separate the pulp from the skin and seeds. Place the pulp with the remaining cup of water in the saucepan. Add the pouch of spices, salt and turmeric. Cook for about 30 minutes on medium low. Add the panir cubes and fenugreek leaves. Cook for another 15 minutes. Remove the pouch.

In a separate pan, heat the butter and sauté the peppers on medium low for 3 to 4 minutes. Stir the paprika and green and red peppers into the sauce. Simmer about 10 to 15 minutes. Add the half-and-half or cream. Cook the mixture on low to heat through; do not allow the sauce to boil. Add the garam masala and serve.

Alu Palak Bhaji
(Potatoes with Spinach)

3 tablespoons mustard oil or canola oil
Small pinch asafoetida (optional)
2 to 3 dry red chilies
2 teaspoons panch pooran [page xviii]
4 cups new potatoes, cut in ¾ inch cubes
8 cups fresh spinach, finely chopped
1 to 1½ teaspoons salt

Heat a heavy 12 inch skillet on medium high. Add the oil and heat it for about 1 minute. Remove the skillet from the heat and add the asafoetida and chilies. (If you prefer the dish hot, break each chili into two or three pieces.) Add the panch pooran. When it sizzles, stir in the potatoes.

Return the skillet to the heat. Turn the heat to medium and sauté the potatoes for 5 to 7 minutes. They should be coated with the oil lightly crusted.

Add the spinach and salt and stir to combine. Cover the pan and cook for another 5 to 7 minutes, stirring once.

Remove the lid. If there is too much moisture, turn the heat up for a few minutes to evaporate the excess. Reduce the heat to low and cook for a few more minutes, until the potatoes are tender.

Sukhi Moong Dal
(Dry Moong Dal)

2 cups moong dal
2 tablespoons oil
1 teaspoon cumin seeds
1 teaspoon ground cumin
1 teaspoon ground coriander
½ teaspoon turmeric
1 teaspoon cayenne or paprika
1½ teaspoons salt
2 cups water
1 teaspoon garam masala
2 lemons, thinly sliced
Chopped cilantro

Pick over the dal and soak it for two to six hours. Wash, rinse and drain the soaked dal.

Heat a heavy 4 quart saucepan or skillet on medium high. Add the oil and the cumin seeds. As soon as they begin to sizzle, add the ground cumin, coriander, turmeric and cayenne. Stir in the drained dal and cook for about 5 minutes, stirring frequently.

Stir in the salt and water and bring to a boil. Reduce the heat to medium low; stir. Cover the pot and simmer for 20 minutes. The water should evaporate, and the dal should be tender.

Turn off the heat. Sprinkle on the garam masala and fluff with a fork. Cover the pan and let the dal stand for about five minutes before serving. Squeeze juice of a lemon into dal and serve.

Garnish with lemon slices and cilantro.

Menu 14
[Serves 8 to 10 persons]

Dal Ghia (Chana Dal with White Gourd or Zucchini)

Bharva Bhindi (Stuffed Okra)

Navratan Bhaji (Mixed Vegetables)

Paratha or Chapatis

Plain Yogurt

This dal with gourd has been cooked in our family for as long as I can remember. As a little girl, I never liked it, but as I grew up and started using the other vegetable side dishes of my own choosing, the dal began to taste better and better. You may cook the dal in advance and make the baghar just before serving.

Dal Ghia
(Chana Dal with White Gourd or Zucchini)

1½ pounds white gourd or zucchini, peeled and cut into
¾ to 1 inch cubes (about 4 cups)
2 teaspoons oil
1 teaspoon cumin seeds
1 tablespoon minced ginger
2 cups chana dal, cleaned and soaked in water for 2 to 3 hrs.
¾ teaspoon turmeric
1 finely chopped green chili
1½ teaspoons salt
6 cups water

For baghar:
2 to 3 tablespoons butter or oil
1 medium sized onion, finely chopped
2 medium tomatoes, chopped
1 teaspoon paprika
1 teaspoon garam masala

Heat a heavy four quart pot on medium high. Add the oil, cumin and ginger. Sauté, stirring, for a few seconds. Add the dal, turmeric, chili and salt, and sauté for about 5 minutes. Add water and bring to a boil. Reduce the heat to medium, cover and cook for 20 to 30 minutes. The dal should be tender, and the water should be separate from the dal.

Add gourd or zucchini and cook on medium low for 30 minutes. The dal and vegetables should be cooked to an even consistency.

Heat the butter or oil in a small skillet on medium. Sauté the onions until they are golden. Stir in the tomatoes and cook until the fat separates. Stir in the paprika and garam masala and stir the baghar into the dal.

Bharva Bhindi
(Stuffed Okra)

4 cups small tender okra (about 1½ pounds)
2 teaspoons amchur
2 teaspoons ground coriander
1 teaspoon ground cumin
½ teaspoon turmeric
½ teaspoon cayenne
1 teaspoon garam masala
1 teaspoon salt
4-5 tablespoons oil
1 large onion, coarsely sliced

Wash okra and pat dry. Okra should be dry. Trim the tops and make a slit in each pod without cutting it through. Mix all the spices and salt and fill the okra with the spice mixture. Some of the spice mixture will be left over.

Heat the oil in a heavy skillet on medium. Add the onions and okra. Stir gently to coat the vegetables with oil. Cover and cook for about 5 minutes. Uncover and stir in the remaining spices. Cook for another 3-4 minutes, uncovered. Reduce the heat to medium low and sauté until the vegetables are crisp.

Navratan Bhaji
(Nine Mixed Vegetables)

2 cups cauliflower, cut into 1½ inch florets
1 cup broccoli, cut into 1½ inch florets
1 cup carrot sticks, 1½ inches long
4 tablespoons oil
2 cups thinly sliced onions
1 tablespoon minced green chili
1 tablespoon minced ginger
1 teaspoon paprika
1 cup zucchini, cut into 1½ inch sticks
1 cup sugar snap peas, trimmed
1 cup mixed green and red pepper, cut into strips
1 cup tomato sauce
1 to 1½ teaspoons salt
1 to 1½ teaspoons garam masala
1 cup almonds blanched, halved and dry roasted
½ cup minced cilantro

Steam cauliflower, broccoli and carrots until tender but still crunchy.

Heat a large, heavy skillet on medium high and add oil. Add sliced onions, chili, ginger and paprika. Sauté until the onions are transparent and slightly golden, about 5 to 7 minutes.

Add the zucchini sticks and sauté about 5 minutes. Add the sugar snap peas and peppers. Cook on medium high until the liquid evaporates. Stir in the steamed vegetables and cook for 3 to 4 minutes. Add the tomato sauce and salt and simmer for 8 to 10 minutes. Stir in the garam masala, cover and let the mixture sit for a minute.

Garnish with toasted almonds and cilantro.

VEGETARIAN NIRVANA
A PASSAGE TO NORTH INDIAN CUISINE

Menu 15
[Serves 6 to 8 persons]

Raungi (Black-eyed Peas)

Makhani Alu (Creamy Potatoes)

Green Beans with Tomatoes

Palak Raita (Spinach Raita)

Methi Poori (Poori with Fenugreek)

Black-eyed peas are readily available here. In India, we always got the dry variety, but when I discovered frozen black-eyed peas, they turned out to be even better. The creamy potatoes and green beans make a very appetizing combination with the dry-cooked dal.

Raungi
(Black-eyed Peas)

3 10-ounce packages of frozen black-eyed peas
1 teaspoon salt
½ teaspoon ground ginger
1 cup water
2 to 3 tablespoons oil
1 teaspoon whole cumin seeds
1 medium onion, chopped
2 tablespoons fresh ginger, finely chopped
2 teaspoons ground cumin
2 teaspoons ground coriander
½ teaspoon cayenne
1 teaspoon garam masala
2 teaspoons amchur powder or juice of 1 lemon or 1 lime
Chopped cilantro for garnish

In a saucepan, combine black-eyed peas, salt, ginger and 1cup water. Bring to boil on high. Reduce heat to medium. Cook, covered, for about 10-15 minutes. Turn the heat off and leave the pot on the stove for another 10 minutes. Ensure that beans are tender.

In a skillet, heat the oil on medium high. Add the cumin seeds and let them sizzle and darken. Stir in the onions and fresh ginger and sauté until the onions are light golden brown.

Add the cumin and coriander and cook for 1 to 2 minutes. Add the cayenne, garam masala and amchur powder or lemon juice.

Stir the baghar into the black-eyed peas. Serve hot, garnished with chopped cilantro.

Makhani Alu
(Creamy Potatoes)

1 large or 2 small onions, coarsely chopped
2 inch piece fresh ginger
1 jalapeño or green chili
2 cups 2% milk
3 tablespoons lemon juice
½ teaspoon turmeric
1 teaspoon paprika
1 teaspoon ground coriander
1 teaspoon ground cumin
1½ teaspoons salt or to taste
4 tablespoons vegetable oil
20-24 small potatoes (walnut size)
1 teaspoon garam masala
Cilantro for garnish

Mince onions, ginger and jalapeño or green chili in a food processor.

In a heavy 12" skillet, combine milk, lemon juice, turmeric, paprika, coriander, salt and onion mixture. Add the potatoes and marinate for about 1 hour.

Bring the mixture to a boil on medium high. Add oil. Reduce the heat to medium low. Cover and cook for about 20 to 25 minutes, stirring frequently. When the potatoes are tender, turn up the heat and cook, uncovered, to evaporate the excess liquid. The sauce should thicken and coat the potatoes.

Sprinkle with garam masala and gently stir in. Garnish with chopped cilantro.

Haree Phali aur Tamatar
(Green Beans with Tomatoes)

2 tablespoons vegetable oil
1 teaspoon cumin seeds
¼ cup finely chopped onion
½ teaspoon turmeric
½ teaspoon cayenne
1 teaspoon salt
1 pound fresh green beans, cut into ½" pieces
½ cup finely chopped tomatoes
½ teaspoon garam masala

Heat the oil in a 3-quart heavy saucepan on medium. When the oil is hot, add the cumin seeds and onions. Sauté until the onions are light gold in color. Add the turmeric, cayenne, salt and green beans. Stir to coat the beans with the spices. Cover the pan and reduce the heat to medium low. Cook for about 10 minutes or until the beans are a little tender.

Stir in the tomatoes and raise the heat to medium. Cook for 5-7 minutes until the tomatoes are tender. Cook uncovered for a few minutes to evaporate excess moisture, if necessary. Add the garam masala just before serving.

Menu 16
[Serves 6 to 8 persons]

Methi Chaman Khumbi (Spinach and Fenugreek with Mushrooms)

Zucchini with Tomatoes

Karahi Panir (Panir Cooked in a Wok)

Matar Pulao (Rice with Peas)

Mint and Sweet Onion Raita

Potato Kulcha or Parathas

This unusual combination of spinach and fenugreek with mushrooms is one of my trial-and-error creations. Karahi panir is a quick and nutritious dish to complement the spinach. This menu has become a family favorite.

Methi Chaman Khumbi
(Spinach and Fenugreek with Mushrooms)

¼ cup water
6 cups chopped spinach (about 1½ pounds)
¾ cup dry fenugreek *OR* 2 cups fresh fenugreek leaves
2 green chilies, chopped
4 tablespoons vegetable oil
½ cup onions, finely chopped
8 ounces mushrooms, sliced
1 teaspoon paprika
¾ teaspoon salt
¼ cup heavy cream

In a heavy-based pot, combine water, spinach, fenugreek and chilies. Cook on medium until the spinach is tender, about 10 minutes. Cool and puree.

In a skillet, heat the oil on medium. Add the onions and sauté until they are light gold in color. Add the mushrooms and paprika. Raise the heat to medium high to cook the mushrooms quickly without releasing too much moisture. The mushrooms should take about 5 minutes to cook.

Stir in the salt and pureed greens. Stirring continuously, cook on medium heat to evaporate the extra moisture.

Add the cream and heat through.

Zucchini with Tomatoes and Onions

2-3 tablespoons oil
1 medium onion, sliced
1 green chili
¾ teaspoon ground cumin
¾ teaspoon ground coriander
2 pounds small zucchini, sliced ¼ inch thick
½ teaspoon turmeric
1 teaspoon salt
2 large tomatoes, finely chopped
1 teaspoon garam masala
1 tablespoon chopped cilantro

In a heavy skillet, heat the oil on medium. Add onion and chili and sauté until the onions are golden brown. Add the cumin, coriander, zucchini, turmeric and salt. Mix well, cover and cook for 3 to 4 minutes.

Add the tomatoes and cook, uncovered, on medium until the tomatoes are tender and the zucchini is cooked. Sprinkle with garam masala and garnish with cilantro.

Karahi Panir
(Panir Cooked in a Wok)

2 teaspoons coriander seeds
1 or 2 dried red chilies
4 tablespoons oil
1 medium onion, thinly sliced
1 or 2 green chilies, minced (optional)
1½ inch piece fresh ginger, minced
1 bell pepper, cut into long strips, ½ inch wide
1 red sweet pepper, cut into long strips, ½ inch wide
2 large tomatoes, finely chopped
Panir made from 1 gallon 2% milk, cut into 2" x ½"x ½" pieces
    [pp: xxi-xxii]
¾ to 1 teaspoon salt
¼ cup cilantro, finely chopped

In a skillet, dry roast the coriander seeds and red chilies until they are slightly crisp. Crush them on a cutting board with a rolling pin. Heat the oil in a wok. Add the sliced onions, green chilies and ginger. Sauté until onions turn pink on the edges. Add red and green pepper slices and sauté for a couple of minutes.

Add the chopped tomatoes and cook until the tomatoes are tender. Stir in the panir slices, coriander seeds and red chilies and salt. Mix well. Cover and cook on medium low for about 7 to 10 minutes. Sprinkle with chopped cilantro.

Menu 17

Menu 17
[Serves 8 to 10 persons]

Khoya Matar (Peas with Crumbled Panir and Cashews)

Rajmah (Red Kidney Beans)

Masaledar Alu (Spicy Potatoes)

Broccoli with Mushrooms

Gajjar Pulao (Rice with Carrots)

Cucumber Raita

Chapatis or Poodina Kulcha

Rajmah, Pulao and Masaledar Alu was my all-time favorite meal in childhood. My children also learned to love this menu. Every time they are home, this meal is a must. To increase its nutritional value, I added the Broccoli and Mushrooms, which has been a welcome addition. Khoya Matar accompanies the meal to make it more elaborate and festive.

Khoya Matar
(Peas with Crumbled Panir)

1 cup powdered milk
Panir made out of 1 gallon 2% milk, crumbled [Page xxi-xxii]
2 tablespoons minced ginger
1 green chili, minced
4—5 tablespoons oil
¾ cup raw cashews
½ to1 teaspoon cayenne or 1 teaspoon paprika
3 large tomatoes, finely chopped, or 16 ounces
canned tomatoes, crushed
28 ounces frozen green peas
1½ teaspoons cumin seeds, dry roasted and ground
2 teaspoons coriander seeds, dry roasted and ground
1 teaspoon garam masala
½ cup cilantro, chopped
1 teaspoon salt or to taste

Pour the powdered milk into a large, heavy skillet and cook, stirring continuously, on low heat for 5 to 7 minutes. The powdered milk should turn slightly pink. Make sure that the milk does not get too dark. Now add the crumbled panir and mix thoroughly.

Heat a large skillet on medium. Add the oil and the minced ginger and chili. Sauté for 2 to 3 minutes. Add the cashews and fry them for a minute. Now add the cayenne or paprika and tomatoes. Cook until the oil separates. Add the peas and salt and cook for a few minutes, stirring occasionally. Add the panir mixture and half of the cilantro and simmer for 10 minutes. If it sticks to the bottom, add a little water. The dish should look like scrambled eggs. Sprinkle in the roasted ground cumin/coriander seeds and garam masala. Stir gently and garnish with the rest of the cilantro.

Rajmah
(Red Kidney Beans)

2 cups red kidney beans
7 cups water
2 teaspoons salt
1 teaspoon ground ginger
2 bay leaves
4 to 6 whole cloves
2-3 cloves of garlic
1 medium onion, chopped
¼ cup tamarind pulp [Page xviii] or 3 tablespoons lemon juice

For baghar:
4 to 6 tablespoons vegetable oil
1 teaspoon whole cumin seeds
1½ inch fresh ginger, scraped and finely chopped
1 medium onion, chopped
1 teaspoon ground cumin
1 teaspoon ground coriander
1 teaspoon cayenne or 1 jalapeño, finely chopped
2 teaspoons garam masala
¼ cup chopped cilantro

Pick over and wash the kidney beans and put them in a crock pot. Add the water and soak them overnight. In the morning add salt, ginger, bay leaves, cloves, garlic and onion, and cook on high for 5 to 6 hours. Make sure that Rajmah are tender, if not, cook them until they are quite tender. Stir in the tamarind pulp and let the dal simmer while you make the baghar.

In a medium-sized saucepan, heat the oil on medium high. Add the cumin seeds. They will sizzle and darken immediately if the oil is hot enough. Add the ginger and onions and stir to coat with oil. Sauté, stirring frequently, until the onions are golden brown. Stir in the remaining spices. Cook on medium, covered, stirring frequently.

Stir the baghar into the kidney beans. Simmer for another 15 minutes and serve hot, garnished with chopped cilantro.

Masaledar Alu
(Spicy Potatoes)

1½ Lbs small red or new white potatoes, washed but not peeled
4 tablespoons oil
1 teaspoon whole cumin seeds
1 teaspoon mustard seeds
2 teaspoons ground coriander
1 teaspoon ground cumin
1 dried red chili (broken in half if you prefer the dish hot)
1 to1½ teaspoons salt or to taste
1 teaspoon garam masala
1 teaspoon amchur (omit if not available)

Cut the potatoes into 1 inch pieces, about 4 to 6 pieces per potato.

Heat oil to smoking in a heavy, large skillet. Remove from heat. Add cumin and mustard seeds and cook, covered, until the mustard seeds stop popping. Add the red chili and return the skillet to medium heat.

Add the potatoes, salt, ground cumin and coriander. Stir and mix well so that each piece is well coated with the spices. Cover and steam cook on medium low heat for 5 to 8 minutes. Uncover and sauté until the potatoes are cooked through and are crispy.

Add the garam masala and amchur powder. Mix gently and thoroughly and serve.

Broccoli with Mushrooms

½ pound mushrooms
1 pound broccoli
2-3 tablespoons oil
1 teaspoon whole cumin seeds
1 teaspoon mustard seeds
2 whole dried red chili
¾ teaspoon salt

Clean and slice the mushrooms. Wash the broccoli and cut into small florets. Peel the stems and slice ½" thick.

In a heavy skillet, heat oil to smoking. Remove from heat and stir in the cumin seeds, mustard seeds and chili. Cover the pan until the mustard seeds have stopped popping.

Reduce the heat to medium. Put the pan back on the heat and stir in the mushrooms. Sauté for a couple of minutes.

Reduce the heat to low. Stir in the broccoli, add salt, stir and cover. Cook for 5 minutes.

Uncover the pan and raise the heat to medium high. Gently stir the vegetables until the moisture evaporates and still crisp. Lower the heat and sauté for a few more minutes, stirring frequently. Serve immediately.

Note: *This dish tastes best when served freshly cooked. Reheating subtracts from the fresh flavor.*

Menu 18
[Serves 8 to 10 Persons]

Kashmiri Rajmah (Red Kidney Beans, Kashmiri Style)

Bharva Mirch (Stuffed Peppers)

Surkh Panir (Panir in Red Sauce)

Haak Saag (Swiss Chard)

Plain Rice

I have included some Kashmiri menus in this book. My family had many relatives living in Jammu and Kashmir, and they introduced us to vegetarian Kashmiri cuisine, which we all enjoyed. It adds a different dimension to other styles of North Indian cuisine. In particular, Kashmiri cooking features three flavors that differ from those used in North Indian cuisine, i.e., mustard oil, ground ginger and ground fennel. Rice, rather than wheat, is the staple starch.

Kashmiri Rajmah
(Red Kidney Beans, Kashmiri Style)

2 cups small red kidney beans
7 cups water
3 onions, coarsely chopped
2 cloves garlic
3-4 green chilies, chopped (optional)
1½ teaspoons salt
1½ tablespoons canola oil
1½ tablespoons mustard oil
1 teaspoon whole cumin seeds
2 tablespoons ginger root, minced
1½ teaspoons ground coriander
½ teaspoon cayenne
2 teaspoons ground fennel
½ teaspoon ground ginger
4-6 green cardamoms, crushed
2" cinnamon stick
1 teaspoon sugar
¼ cup tamarind pulp [page xviii]
1 cup pureed tomatoes
½ cup cilantro, chopped

Pick, wash and soak the beans overnight in 7 cups water. Cook the beans in their soaking water with onions, garlic, green chilies and salt, until they are quite tender (15-20 minutes in the pressure cooker, 4 hours in the crock pot or 1 to 1½ hour on the stove). As the beans begin to boil vigorously, turn the heat to medium low.

Heat both oils together and add the cumin seeds. When they begin to splatter, add the minced ginger and sauté for a minute or so. Stir in ground coriander, cayenne, fennel, ground ginger, cardamoms, cinnamon and sugar. Stir in the tamarind pulp and tomatoes. Cook the mixture until the oil begins to separate. Combine with the cooked beans and simmer for 30 minutes. You may have to add a little water if the beans become too thick.

Stir in half the cilantro; garnish with the remainder.

Bharva Mirch
(Stuffed Peppers)

This dish includes two stuffings;panir and potatoes, and is served with a sauce of onions and tomatoes.

4 medium bell peppers
2 large boiled white potatoes
1 tablespoon minced fresh ginger
1 teaspoon ground cumin
1 teaspoon ground coriander
¼ teaspoon garam masala
½ teaspoon salt
1½ cups crumbled panir [pp: xxi-xxii]
2 scallions, finely chopped
1 green chili, minced (optional)
¼ teaspoon salt
¼ teaspoon freshly ground black pepper
2 tablespoons oil

Sauce:
1 teaspoon cumin seeds
1 teaspoon coriander seeds
1 teaspoon fennel seeds
4 to 5 tablespoons oil
1 cup minced onion
2 tablespoons minced fresh ginger
1 teaspoon lemon juice
1 large ripe tomato, peeled and chopped
1 teaspoon salt
½ teaspoon cayenne
½ teaspoon paprika
1 cup tomato sauce
½ cup yogurt
½ cup cilantro, finely chopped
2 tablespoons oil

Wash and dry the bell peppers and cut them in half. Remove the seeds and membranes.

Grate the boiled potatoes and add cumin and coriander powder, garam masala and salt.

Mix the panir with the scallions, green chili, salt and pepper. Divide the potato mixture and the panir mixture into eight portions. Fill each pepper half first with the panir mixture and then with the potato mixture. Set aside.

For the sauce*:* Dry roast and grind the cumin, coriander and fennel seeds and set aside. Heat the oil over medium in a heavy saucepan. Add the minced onions and ginger and sauté until the onions are golden in color. Add the tomato and cook until the tomato is soft and the oil begins to separate. Stir in all the spices and lemon juice and add the tomato sauce. Reduce the heat to medium low and cook for about ten minutes. Stir in the beaten yogurt and half the cilantro. Bring to the boil and remove from the heat.

In a heavy skillet, heat 2 tablespoons oil on medium low. Put the peppers into the pan, potato side down. Cover and cook slowly, checking often to ensure that they don't burn. The potatoes should be crusty and golden. Turn and cook the other side until the pepper shells are tender.

Arrange the cooked peppers on a platter. Spoon the sauce over them and garnish with the remaining cilantro.

Panir Surkh
(Panir in Red Sauce)

Panir made from 1 gallon of milk, cut in 1 x 2 inch pieces, fried and soaked [pp xxi-xxii]

2 tablespoons vegetable oil

2 tablespoons mustard oil

1 teaspoon cumin seeds

2 green chilies, finely chopped

1 teaspoon paprika

1 teaspoon ground ginger

4 teaspoons ground fennel seeds

1 teaspoon salt

1 cup pureed tomatoes

1 tablespoon tamarind pulp [page xviii]

½ cup water

1 teaspoon garam masala

Heat both oils in a large, heavy skillet on medium heat. Add the cumin seeds and green chilies; stir and add the paprika, ginger, fennel seeds and salt. Stir in the tomatoes and tamarind pulp.

Cook until the oil begins to separate, about 10-15 minutes. Stir in the drained panir and water. When it starts to cook vigorously, turn the heat down to medium low and let it simmer for about 10 minutes. Stir in the garam masala and serve.

75

Haak Saag
(Swiss Chard)

1½ pounds Swiss chard
6 to 8 scallions
3 tablespoons mustard oil or vegetable or canola oil
Small pinch asafoetida (optional)
2 or 3 dry red chilies
1 or 2 green chilies, chopped
1 teaspoon salt

Wash the Swiss chard and scallions to remove all grit. Chop the chard coarsely and the scallions finely.

Heat the oil in a large wok or heavy skillet on medium high. As soon as the oil begins to smoke a little, remove it from the heat, let it cool a little and add the asafoetida and dried red chilies. (Mustard oil is a little pungent; it is important to heat the oil to smoking and then cool.) Add the scallions, chard, green chilies and salt and mix well. Cover the pan and reduce the heat to medium. Cook for five minutes, stir and cook for another 5 to 7 minutes or until tender.

Menu 19
[Serves 6 to 8 persons]

Madre Maa (Whole Urd, Kashmiri Style)

Kashmiri Dum Alu (Potatoes in Yogurt, Kashmiri Style)

Sok Vangum (Kashmiri Eggplant)

Plain Rice

This whole Urd dal is very different from Makhani Urd, but it tastes wonderful. The first time I tried it, I fell in love with it. Kashmiri Dum Alu (whole potatoes in sauce) is delicious. You must try this menu to see the difference. Kashmiri food is normally more oily and hot and usually is eaten with plain rice. I have tried to reduce the oil and make these recipes less hot.

Madre Maa
(Whole Urd, Kashmiri Style)

1½ cups whole urd
3-4 green chilies
½ teaspoon ground ginger
¾ teaspoon turmeric
1 teaspoon salt
1 tablespoon mustard oil
1 tablespoon canola oil
1 teaspoon cumin seeds
½ teaspoon cayenne
1 teaspoon ground coriander
20 almonds, blanched and sliced
1½ cups sour yogurt, beaten smooth
¾ teaspoon garam masala
½ cup raisins

Wash and soak the dal in 6 cups water for overnight. Cook the dal with the chilies, ground ginger, turmeric and salt. The dal can be cooked in a pressure cooker (about 15 minutes), crock pot (about 4 to 6 hours) or on the stove (1 hour on medium heat). The dal should be cooked long enough so that the beans and water combine into a creamy consistency. If you use a pressure cooker, cook the dal until tender and finish cooking on the stove on very low heat.

Heat the oils together in small saucepan on medium high. Let the oils become very hot. Remove from the stove and cool the oils a little. Add cumin seeds, cayenne, ground coriander, almonds, yogurt and garam masala. Return to medium heat. Add raisins and heat through. It may take 3 to 4 minutes. Stir into the beans and simmer for 15 to 20 minutes.

Kashmiri Dum Alu
(Potatoes in Yogurt, Kashmiri Style)

20—24 small potatoes (about walnut size)
Vegetable oil for deep frying
1½ cups yogurt, preferably sour
2—3 tablespoons vegetable oil OR
(1 tablespoon mustard oil and 2 tablespoons vegetable oil)
1 to 1½ teaspoons salt
4 teaspoons ground fennel
1 teaspoon ground ginger
1½ teaspoons paprika
½ teaspoon cayenne pepper
1½ teaspoons garam masala
1 to 2 teaspoons amchur (optional)
1½ cups water

Boil the potatoes in salted water until their skins can be peeled off easily. Do not overcook them. Drain and cool thoroughly. Fry the potatoes in hot oil until golden. Cool them and prick them all over with a fork or sharp knife.

Beat the yogurt until smooth. Add all of the spices. (If the yogurt is a few days old or is on the tart side, the amchur may be omitted.)

Heat the oil and add the yogurt mixture. Now add the fried potatoes and half the water. Cook on medium high. When the mixture begins to cook rapidly, reduce the heat to medium low and cook until the oil starts to come on top. Stir and add another the rest of the water and cook until the sauce thickens and the oil starts to float. Serve with plain rice or chapatis.

Sok Vangun
(Kashmiri Eggplant)

1 large eggplant, about 1½ pound
2 cups oil for deep frying
1 tablespoon mustard oil
1 tablespoon canola oil
¾ teaspoon salt
1 teaspoon cumin seeds
¾ teaspoon ground ginger
3 teaspoons ground fennel
½ teaspoon garam masala
½ teaspoon cayenne
2-3 tablespoons tamarind pulp

Cut the eggplant in half lengthwise and slice each ½ inch thick. Heat the oil and fry the eggplant until the slices are golden. Drain on a paper towel. (Alternatively, the eggplant slices may be coated with oil and broiled or roasted in a 475° oven for 20 minutes.)

Heat the mustard and canola oils in a heavy skillet on high. Fry the cumin seeds until they begin to splatter. Stir in the ginger, fennel, garam masala, cayenne and salt. Stir in the eggplant slices and tamarind pulp. Cover the pan, reduce the heat to low and simmer 5 to 7 minutes.

Menu 20
[Serves 6 to 8 persons]

Bharva Baingan (Kashmiri Stuffed Eggplant)

Panir Zarda (Panir in Yellow Sauce)

Kashmiri Khumbi (Mushrooms, Kashmiri Style)

Khamiri Poori (Leavened Fried Bread)

Plain Rice

Small round eggplants are becoming more readily available in farmers markets and Asian markets. If you cannot find them, you can substitute small, long Asian eggplants. Panir Zarda is a thin sauce with panir cubes. Many kinds of mushrooms grow wild in Kashmir. This dish is an interesting way of cooking a combination of mushrooms.

Bharva Baingan
(Kashmiri Stuffed Eggplant)

1½ lbs round or small oriental eggplants
1½ teaspoons salt for sprinkling
1 large onion, grated
1 inch piece ginger root, grated
2 large tomatoes, very finely chopped
1½ tablespoons mustard oil
1½ tablespoons canola oil
3 teaspoons ground fennel
¾ teaspoon ground ginger
½ teaspoon cayenne
½ teaspoon garam masala
½ cup water

Cut the eggplant in quarters without cutting through the stem. Sprinkle the inside of the eggplant with a little salt and let it drain in a colander until the masala is ready.

Heat the oils in a heavy skillet on medium high and stir in the finely minced ginger and onion. Cook until the onions are golden in color. Add chopped tomatoes and cook until the oil begins to separate. Add fennel, ground ginger, cayenne, salt and garam masala. Remove from heat and cool.

Gently wipe off the eggplant. Fill with the masala, reserving about two tablespoon. Add ½ cup water to the reserved masala. Put the stuffed eggplant in the skillet and stir gently. Cook on low, basting with the sauce, until the eggplant is tender and nearly all the sauce is absorbed.

Panir Zarda
(Panir in Yellow Sauce)

Panir made from 1 gallon 2% milk [pages xxi-xxii]
2 tablespoons oil
2 tablespoons mustard oil
2-3 bay leaves
1 teaspoon turmeric
½ teaspoon cayenne pepper
½ teaspoon paprika
1 teaspoon ground ginger
4 teaspoons ground fennel seeds
6 to 8 green cardamoms
1 teaspoon salt
1 cup sour yogurt
2 cups milk
1 teaspoon garam masala
2 cups canola oil for frying

Cut the panir into pieces about 2" x 1" x 1". Fry the pieces and soak them in boiling water for 30 to 45 minutes.

In a heavy saucepan, heat both oils on medium high until smoking. Remove from heat and let it cool a little before you add the spices. Add bay leaves, turmeric, cayenne, paprika, ginger, fennel, cardamoms and salt. Return the pan to the heat. Beat the yogurt into milk and add to the spices. Bring to a boil. Reduce the heat to medium low.

Drain the panir and stir into the sauce. Bring to the boil again; reduce heat and simmer about 10 minutes. Sprinkle the garam masala and turn heat off.

Kashmiri Khumbi
(Mushrooms, Kashmiri Style)

4 tablespoons canola oil
1 tablespoon mustard oil (optional)
4 to 6 cloves of garlic, minced
1½" piece of fresh ginger, minced
1 medium onion, minced
3 cups tomatoes, skinned and finely chopped
4 teaspoons ground fennel seed
1 teaspoon ground ginger
1 teaspoon cayenne pepper *or* ½ teaspoon cayenne and
    teaspoon paprika
1 teaspoon salt
1 pound button mushrooms, chopped into ½" pieces
1 pound Shiitake, Portobello or other mushrooms, chopped into
½ to ¾ inch pieces
½ teaspoon garam masala

Heat both the oils in a large, heavy skillet on medium. Add the minced garlic and ginger and sauté for a minute or two. Stir in the onion and sauté until light golden in color. Add tomatoes. Cook the mixture until the tomatoes are tender and the oil begins to separate. Stir in the fennel, ginger, cayenne, paprika and salt.

Stir the mushrooms into the cooked masala. The mushrooms will give off moisture. Raise the heat to medium high and cook uncovered, stirring often, for about 5 to 7 minutes.

Stir in the garam masala and serve.

Menu 21
[Serves 6 to 8 persons]

Phool Gobi aur Pyaz (Cauliflower with Onions)

Kadhi

Phali aur Gajjar Bhaji (Green Beans and Carrots)

Plain Rice

Parathas or Moong Dal Parathas

Kadhi is popular in all parts of India. Every region has its own version. It is made out of gram flour and yogurt. In North India, kadhi is quite thick and often contains dumplings or vegetables.

Phool Gobi aur Pyaz
(Cauliflower with Onions)

1 large head of cauliflower
4 to 6 tablespoons oil
1 teaspoon whole cumin seeds
1 large onion, thinly sliced
1½ inch piece of fresh ginger, finely chopped
½ teaspoon turmeric
1 teaspoon ground coriander
1 teaspoon ground cumin
½ teaspoon cayenne pepper (optional)
1 teaspoon salt
1 teaspoon garam masala
¼ cup finely chopped cilantro

Wash the cauliflower and cut it into 1½inch florets.

Heat the oil in a heavy skillet or saucepan. Add the cumin seeds. They will darken in a few seconds. Stir in the onion and ginger and sauté until the onion is golden.

Add the cauliflower, turmeric, coriander, cumin, cayenne and salt. Stir until the florets are evenly coated with the spices. Cover the pan and reduce the heat to low.

Cook approximately 10 to 15 minutes until the cauliflower is tender, stirring frequently. If there is any excess moisture in the pan, raise the heat to high and cook, stirring frequently, until the moisture has evaporated.

Add the garam masala and mix well. Garnish with chopped cilantro.

Kadhi
(Buttermilk and Gram Flour Curry)

For pakoras:

¾ cup gram flour

½ cup water

½ cup finely chopped onions

1 tablespoon dry fenugreek leaves

¼ teaspoon salt

¼ teaspoon cayenne pepper

Oil for deep frying

Mix all the ingredients except oil and beat the batter until smooth and light.
Heat the oil on medium in a wok. Drop the batter into the hot oil a teaspoonful at a time, and fry the pakoras until they are golden.

For kadhi:

8 ounces sour yogurt

½ cup gram flour

3 cups water

3 tablespoons oil

½ teaspoon cumin seeds

½ teaspoon fenugreek seeds

½ cup chopped onions

¼ teaspoon turmeric

½ teaspoon cayenne pepper

1 teaspoon salt

½ teaspoon garam masala

Mix the yogurt and gram flour and add the water gradually. The batter should be smooth.

Heat 2 tablespoons oil in a 4-quart saucepan on medium high. Add the cumin and fenugreek seeds. As soon as they begin to sizzle, add onions and sauté until they are golden. Now add turmeric, cayenne and salt. Pour the batter into the saucepan. Cook, stirring constantly, until it starts to cook. Turn the heat down to medium low and let it simmer until the oil rises to the top of the kadhi. It may take from 45 minutes to an hour.

Stir in the pakoras and cook for another five minutes. Stir in the garam masala.

Note: *If you don't want to fry pakoras, you can substitute vegetables like cauliflower, red or green peppers or potatoes. After the onions are golden in color, add 1½ cups of vegetables of your choice, cut into 1 inch pieces. Stir fry for a couple of minutes.*

Phali aur Gajjar Bhaji
(Green Beans and Carrots)

12 oz. tender green beans
8 oz. baby carrots
4 tablespoons canola or vegetable oil
2 dry red chilies
4 scallions (1 cup thinly sliced)
¾ teaspoon ground cumin
¾ teaspoon ground coriander
¾ teaspoon salt
1½ teaspoons honey
2 tablespoons lime juice
3 tablespoons roasted pine nuts
½ teaspoon freshly ground black pepper
1 green chili, finely chopped (optional)
¼ cup chopped cilantro

Cut the green beans into pieces about two inches long and the baby carrots in half. Put the beans and carrots and in boiling water. As soon as they are just tender, drain them and place them in a bowl of iced water.

Heat the oil in a heavy skillet on a medium high. Add the red chilies and chopped scallions. Sauté until the scallions are translucent. Add the cumin and coriander and the drained beans and carrots. Add salt. Mix well. Lower the heat to medium. Cover and cook for 5 to 7 minutes. *Do not* let the vegetables *overcook*.

Mix the honey and lime juice and stir into the vegetables. Add pine nuts and black pepper. Add the finely chopped green chili and garnish with cilantro.

Menu 22
[Serves 6 to 8 persons]

Tariwale Chana (Chick Peas in a Light Gravy)

Dum Alu (Potatoes, North Indian Style)

Shahi Gobi (Cauliflower Cooked in a Creamy Sauce)

Boondi Raita

Naan or Methi Parathas

This chana dish was served frequently in Punjab Jain families, but it did not include onions and tomatoes. I used to make excuses not to eat this dish. Later, I tried to improve on it and discovered that it was delicious. With the addition of Dum Alu and Shahi Gobi, it is a royal menu that everyone will enjoy.

Tariwale Chana
(Chick Peas in a Light Gravy)

1¼ cups chick peas
1 teaspoons vegetable oil
½ teaspoon cumin seeds
½ teaspoon turmeric
½ teaspoon cayenne
1 teaspoon salt
6 cups water
¾ cup yogurt, beaten smooth

For baghar:

   3 tablespoons ghee or oil
   1 small onion, chopped
   1 tablespoon fresh ginger, peeled and minced
   2 medium tomatoes, finely chopped
   ½ teaspoon paprika
   1 teaspoon garam masala
   2 tablespoons cilantro, finely chopped

Pick over the chick peas. Soak them overnight in 4 cups water. Drain well.

In a large, heavy pot, heat the oil on medium high. When the oil is hot, add the cumin seeds. They should sizzle and darken almost immediately. Stir in the drained chick peas, turmeric and cayenne.

Add salt and water and raise the heat to high. Bring to a boil. Reduce the heat to medium low. Cover the pot and cook, covered, for 1 to 1½ hours or until the chana is as tender as boiled potatoes.

Stir in the beaten yogurt. Simmer while you prepare the baghar.

For the baghar:

In a small skillet, heat the ghee or oil. Sauté the onion and ginger until golden brown, stirring frequently. Stir in the finely chopped tomatoes and cook until the oil begins to separate. Add the paprika and garam masala and stir the baghar into the chana. Garnish with cilantro.

Dum Alu
(Potatoes with sauce, North Indian Style)

1 teaspoon cumin seeds

1½ teaspoons coriander seeds

½ teaspoon peppercorns

5 to 6 whole cloves

1" cinnamon stick

6 to 8 green cardamoms

2 teaspoons poppy seeds

8 to10 almonds

2 pounds walnut size new potatoes, peeled (or larger potatoes, peeled and cut in half)

2 cups oil for deep frying

1 large onion

1½ inch piece of ginger

1 green chili

6 tablespoons oil

1 teaspoon paprika

½ teaspoon turmeric

1 cup sour yogurt (If the yogurt is not sour, add 1 teaspoon lemon juice or amchur.)

1 to 1½ teaspoons salt

1½ cups water

2 tablespoons cilantro, chopped, for garnish

In a heavy skillet, dry roast the cumin, coriander seeds, peppercorns, cloves, cinnamon stick, cardamoms, poppy seeds and almonds. Cool and grind in a coffee grinder. Boil the potatoes in salted water just long enough so that they can be skinned; they should not be quite tender. Drain and cool. Peel them and deep fry them until they are golden. Let them cool down a little and prick them with fork or sharp knife.

Mince the onion, ginger and chili together. Heat the 6 tablespoons oil in a deep, heavy skillet on medium. Sauté the onion, ginger and chili until the oil begins to separate. Add the ground roasted spices, paprika and turmeric.

Beat the yogurt smooth and add 1 tablespoon yogurt to the onion mixture. Cook on medium low until the moisture evaporates. Continue with the rest of the yogurt, adding 1 tablespoon at a time. Add the salt. Add half the water and the potatoes and cook, covered, until the liquid evaporates. Add the rest of the water and cook until gravy is thick and most of the moisture has dried out. Potatoes will be lightly covered with sauce and spices. Garnish with cilantro.

Shahi Gobi
(Cauliflower Cooked in a Creamy Sauce)

1 large head of cauliflower
2 tablespoons oil
¾ teaspoon cayenne
½ teaspoon ground ginger
¾ teaspoon salt
1 medium onion
2 inch piece of ginger root
2-3 cloves garlic
1 green chili
4 tablespoons oil
1 teaspoon paprika
2 large tomatoes, blanched, peeled and chopped
¾ teaspoon salt
2 large tomatoes, blanched, peeled and pureed
½ cup cilantro, finely chopped
2 tablespoons heavy cream
1 teaspoon garam masala
1 tablespoon oil
½ cup frozen peas

Preheat the oven to 350°. Separate the cauliflower into florets; cut large florets in half if necessary to make each piece no more than 2 inches long and 2 inches wide. Heat a heavy skillet on medium. Add 2 tablespoons oil, cayenne, ground ginger, salt and cauliflower. Sauté for a couple of minutes. Cover the pan and cook 2-3 minutes, until the cauliflower is a little tender but still crunchy. Arrange the cauliflower in a large greased baking dish in a single layer.

To make the sauce, grind the onion, ginger, garlic, and green chili together. Heat the oil in a saucepan on medium high and sauté the mixture on medium until it turns light golden and the oil begins to separate. Add the paprika and chopped tomatoes and cook until the oil begins to separate again. Add salt, pureed tomato and cilantro and bring to a boil. Reduce the heat to low and simmer for about 5 minutes.

Pour three-fourths of the sauce over the cauliflower. Bake for about 30 minutes or until the cauliflower is tender. Add the cream and garam masala to the remaining sauce and pour over the baked cauliflower. Bake for another 5 minutes. In a small pan, heat 1 tablespoon oil and add the peas. Cook them quickly and sprinkle over the baked cauliflower.

Menu 23
[Serves 6 to 8 persons]

Tandoori Sabzi (Grilled Vegetables)

Dal Palak (Dal Cooked with Spinach)

Pulao Masala (Rice with Whole Spices)

Apple Raita

Naan Stuffed with Potatoes

This menu is my own creation based on the Oven-roasted Vegetables. It is the result of my improvising to incorporate broiling or roasting into Indian cooking. In India, meat is roasted in tandoors (clay ovens), but vegetables are not. Dal Palak is a very basic recipe of my mother's with some minor changes.

Tandoori Sabzi
(Grilled Vegetables)

Oil baste:
- ½ cup vegetable oil
- 2 teaspoons black mustard seed
- 2 or 3 green chilies, chopped

Vegetables:
- 1 small cauliflower, cut into 1½ inch florets
- 2 cups new potatoes, cut into 1 inch chunks
- 1 cup carrots, sliced ½ inch thick
- 1 cup zucchini, sliced ½ inch thick
- ½ cup red and green peppers, sliced
- ½ cup quartered onions
- ½ cup mushrooms

Sauce:
- 1 large onion
- 3 hot green chilies
- 1½ inch piece fresh ginger
- 2 large cloves garlic
- 6 tablespoons vegetable oil
- 3 large tomatoes, blanched, skinned and chopped
- 2 teaspoons ground cumin
- 2 teaspoons ground fennel
- 1 teaspoon salt
- ½ teaspoon cayenne pepper
- 1 teaspoon paprika
- ½ cup tomato sauce
- ½ cup slivered almonds, ground
- ½ cup yogurt
- 2 tablespoons sour cream
- 1 teaspoon garam masala
- ½ cup cilantro, chopped

In a small saucepan, cook the oil, mustard seeds and chilies on a very low heat for 10 to 12 minutes. Turn off the heat and let the mixture cool.

Grind the onion, chilies, ginger and garlic in the food processor. Heat the oil in a heavy 3-quart saucepan. Add the ground onions, chilies, ginger and garlic and cook on medium until the oil separates. Stir in the chopped tomatoes and cook until the oil separates again. Stir in the cumin, fennel, salt, cayenne pepper and paprika and cook for 30 seconds or so. Add the tomato sauce and ground almonds and cook for another 5 minutes. Beat the yogurt and sour cream together and stir into the sauce. Heat through.

Coat the vegetables with the chili oil. Put the vegetables in a grill basket or on skewers and grill them for 10 to 12 minutes. You can broil these vegetables or roast them at 400 degrees. Cook the cauliflower, potatoes and carrots for 20-25 minutes; they will take longer to cook. The remaining vegetables should be roasted for 8-10 minutes.

Stir half the chopped cilantro into the sauce and sprinkle the garam masala on top. Garnish with the rest of the cilantro.

Serve the sauce with the grilled vegetables.

Note: *You can substitute eggplant, broccoli, pearl onions or sweet potatoes for the suggested vegetables in this dish.*

Dal Palak
(Dal with Spinach)

1 cup masoor dal
1 tablespoon vegetable oil
1 teaspoon cumin seeds
½ teaspoon cayenne
½ teaspoon turmeric
1 teaspoon salt
3½ cups water
2 cups finely chopped spinach

For the baghar:
3 tablespoons butter or 2 tablespoon ghee
¼ cup onion, finely chopped
½ cup tomato, finely chopped
½ teaspoon paprika
½ teaspoon garam masala
1 tablespoon lime juice

Pick over and wash the dal. Soak it for 2 hours and drain it.

Heat a heavy 3-quart saucepan on medium. Add the oil. Stir in the cumin seeds. As soon as they begin to sizzle, add the cayenne, turmeric and drained dal. Sauté for a couple of minutes. Add the salt and water and bring to the boil. Reduce the heat to medium low. Cover and cook for about 20 minutes. The dal should be tender. Stir in the chopped spinach and cook, covered, for another 30 minutes or so. The dal and spinach should be smooth. If it is not, simmer a little longer.

Heat the ghee or butter in a small saucepan. Add the chopped onions and sauté until they are light golden brown. Add the tomatoes and paprika and cook until the oil begins to separate. Add the garam masala and pour the baghar over the dal. Stir in the baghar and lime juice.

Menu 24
[Serves 6 to 8 persons]

Palak Panir or Ghia Panir Kofta (White Gourd Balls)

Sukhi Urd Chana Dal (Dry-cooked Urd and Chana Dal)

Alu Phali (Dry-cooked Potatoes and Green Beans)

Matar Pulao (Rice with Peas)

Kheera Raita (Cucumber Raita)

Parathas or Poori

Kofta curry is an elaborate dish, but you can make the koftas in advance; they may be kept in the freezer for three or four months. The rest of the menu is quite simple. It should not take much time to prepare.

Palak or Ghia Panir Kofta
(Spinach or White Gourd Balls)

For Koftas:
- 1 to 1¼ cups gram flour
- 1 cup crumbled panir
- 2 cups finely chopped fresh spinach *or* 2 cups grated white gourd
- 1 green chili, finally chopped
- ½ teaspoon salt
- 1 teaspoon ground coriander
- 1 teaspoon ground cumin
- ½ teaspoon cumin seeds
- Oil for deep frying

In a dry skillet, roast the gram flour on low until it darkens slightly and you can smell the roasted aroma. Let it cool down.

Mix the panir, spinach or gourd, green chili and remaining spices. Gradually stir in the gram flour. You may use 1 to 1¼ cups of gram flour, depending upon the moisture content in the panir and spinach or gourd. The dough should be soft and pliable. Form the dough into small balls; you will get 20 to 24 balls.

Heat the oil on medium high. Test the temperature of the oil by dropping in a tiny piece of the kofta mixture. If it starts floating in the oil right away without turning very dark, the oil is ready. Fry a few balls at a time until they are golden brown. Repeat until all are fried.

The kofta may be made ahead of time and frozen. They will keep for three or four months.

For curry:
- 2 medium onions, coarsely chopped
- 1½ inch piece of fresh ginger root, coarsely chopped
- 2 cloves garlic (optional)
- 6 tablespoons oil
- 1 tablespoon butter or ghee (optional)
- ¾ teaspoon turmeric

½ teaspoon cayenne
1 teaspoon paprika
4 large tomatoes, blanched and finely chopped
½ cup yogurt
1½ teaspoons salt
3 cups water
¼ cup heavy cream
1 teaspoon garam masala
Chopped cilantro for garnish

In a food processor, grind the onions, ginger and garlic together. Heat the oil and ghee or butter in a large, heavy saucepan on medium. Fry the ground onion mixture until it turns golden and the oil begins to separate.

Add the turmeric, cayenne, paprika and tomatoes. Cover and cook for five minutes. Uncover the pan and cook until the tomatoes are soft and the oil begins to separate.

Add 1 tablespoon yogurt and cook until the oil begins to separate again. Add the remaining yogurt and cook until the oil begins to separate again, which will take eight minutes or less.

Add the salt and water and bring to the boil. Reduce the heat to medium low and cook for 20 minutes or until the oil begins to float.

Stir in the koftas and bring to the boil. Stir in the cream and cook just until the cream is heated through.

Garnish with cilantro.

Note: *If you are using frozen koftas it will take a little longer for the curry to come to the boil.*

Sukhi Urd and Chana Dal
(Dry Cooked Urd and Chana Dal)

1 cup washed urd dal
3 tablespoons chana dal
1 tablespoon oil
½ teaspoon cumin seeds
1 tablespoon finely chopped fresh ginger
½ teaspoon cayenne
½ teaspoon turmeric
¾ to 1 teaspoon salt
2 cups water

For the baghar:
3 tablespoons oil or ghee
¼ cup chopped onions
½ cup chopped tomatoes
½ teaspoon paprika
½ teaspoon garam masala

Pick over the dal and soak it for 2-3 hours.

Heat a tablespoon of oil in a 3-quart heavy bottomed skillet on medium. Add the cumin seeds. As soon as they begin to sizzle, add the chopped ginger. Stir and cook for a few seconds, and then add cayenne, turmeric and dal. Sauté for 2 to 3 minutes. Add salt and water and bring to a vigorous boil. Reduce the heat to medium low; cover the skillet and cook for 20 to 25 minutes, stirring occasionally. The dal should be tender. If necessary, raise heat to medium and cook to evaporate excess moisture.

Heat the oil or ghee in a small skillet. Add the chopped onions and sauté until they are golden in color. Add the paprika and chopped tomatoes and sauté until the tomatoes are cooked and the oil begins to separate. Add the garam masala. Mix the baghar gently into the dal.

Alu Phali
(Dry-cooked Potatoes and Green Beans)

1 pound fresh green beans
4 medium new potatoes
3-4 tablespoons oil
½ teaspoon black mustard seeds
½ teaspoon cumin seeds
½ teaspoon turmeric
½ teaspoon cayenne
1 teaspoon salt
1 teaspoon roasted ground cumin
1 teaspoon roasted ground coriander
1½ tablespoons lime juice or 1 teaspoon amchur
1 teaspoon garam masala

Wash and trim the beans and cut them into ½ inch pieces. Scrub the potatoes and cut them into ¾ inch pieces.

Heat the oil in a large, heavy skillet on medium. Add the mustard and cumin seeds. As soon as they begin to sizzle, add the potatoes, turmeric and cayenne. Sauté for 3-4 minutes. Add the green beans and salt. Reduce the heat to medium low and cook, covered, for about ten minutes, stirring occasionally so that the vegetables cook evenly. The beans and potatoes should be tender. If there is excess moisture, raise the heat a little to evaporate it. Stir in the ground cumin and coriander, amchur or lime juice and garam masala.

Menu 25

Menu 25
[Serves 8 to 10 persons]

Panjabi Chana (Spicy Dry-cooked whole Chana)

Shahi Baingan (Eggplant Cooked in Yogurt)

Alu aur Panir ki Curry (Panir with Roasted Potato Curry)

Dahi Pakora (Yogurt with Fritters)

Kaju Pulao (Rice with Cashews)

Bhaturas

We used to eat this Chana Bhatura (chick peas and bread) in restaurants frequently and loved it. This dish is always a treat. I kept asking for the recipe, but no one would give me a satisfactory answer. I began experimenting and picking up ideas, and one day I was able to produce good results. This dish has become my specialty in the family, and I am often asked to make it. I hope you will enjoy it, too.

This menu is very elaborate, but you can cut it down to Chana Bhatura and one vegetable, which you can change to your liking, unless you must prepare a banquet.

Panjabi Chana
(Spicy Dry-cooked Chickpeas)

2 tablespoons coriander seeds
1 tablespoon cumin seeds
1 teaspoon black pepper corns
1 teaspoon cloves
8 to 10 green cardamoms
2" cinnamon stick
1 teaspoon ajwain
Dry roast the above spices and grind them to a fine powder.

2 cups dry chick peas (kabuli chana)
¼ teaspoon baking soda
6 cups water
3 or 4 bay leaves
2-3 large cardamoms
1 teaspoon ground ginger
1 teaspoon oil
1 cup tea (1 tea bag brewed in 1 cup water)
2 tablespoons oil
2 tablespoons ghee
¼ cup thinly sliced fresh ginger
2-3 green chilies
1 teaspoon cayenne (optional)
½ cup tamarind pulp *or* ½ cup pomegranate seeds, finely ground
1 tomato, thinly sliced
1 lemon, thinly sliced
¼ cup cilantro, chopped

Pick over the chick peas, wash and soak them in water with baking soda overnight. You can soak the chickpeas in a 4-quart pot and cook them in the same pot.

To the chick peas, add bay leaves, cardamoms, ground ginger, 1 teaspoon oil and tea. The tea is to add a dark color to the chick peas. Bring to a boil on high. As soon as the chick peas come to a hard boil, reduce the heat to medium low. Cover the pot and cook the chick peas until they are tender to the touch, about an hour, depending on the heat. Drain and reserve the cooking liquid.

Mix the ground spices and salt with the boiled and drained chick peas. Mix the ground spices, salt, tamarind or ground pomegranate seeds. Let the mixture stand for at least an hour. (You can do this a day ahead; cool the chick peas to room temperature and refrigerate until ready to use.)

In a large skillet, heat the oil on medium heat. Add the fresh ginger, green chilies, cayenne and chick peas. Mix well and add the reserved liquid little by little. Simmer gently for at least half an hour, stirring gently so that the chick peas keep their shape.

Garnish with tomatoes, lemons and cilantro. Serve with onion relish. [Page 210]

Note: *If you wish chana to be less spicy, then save some of the spice mixture. Taste, and add more spice mixture, if you feel like it.*

Shahi Baingan
(Eggplant Cooked in Yogurt)

2½ pounds eggplant
¾ teaspoon salt
Oil for deep frying
2 large onions, sliced lengthwise
1 teaspoon ground cumin
1 teaspoon ground coriander
½ teaspoon cayenne pepper
½ teaspoon turmeric
¾ teaspoon salt
1 pound chopped tomatoes
6 ounces yogurt
1 teaspoon garam masala
Chopped cilantro for garnish

Halve the eggplant and cut it into ½ inch thick rounds or half rounds. Sprinkle ¾ teaspoon salt on the slices and let the eggplant sit uncovered for 30 minutes. Pat dry with paper towels.

In a deep skillet, heat the oil until nearly smoking. Fry the eggplant slices, a few at a time, until they are golden. Do not crowd them. Drain the fried eggplant slices in a colander. Reserve the drained oil for the next step.

In a skillet, heat 3 to 4 tablespoons oil. Fry the sliced onions until they are golden brown. Add all of the spices except the garam masala. Add the tomatoes and cook on medium, stirring often to prevent sticking, until the oil begins to separate from the tomatoes. Stir in the yogurt and ¾ teaspoon salt and bring the mixture to a boil.

Lower the heat and stir in the eggplant slices and garam masala. Simmer uncovered for 5 minutes. Garnish with cilantro.

Note: *If you do not wish to fry the eggplant, brush the eggplant with oil on both sides, after you pat them dry. Arrange them in a single layer in a cookie sheet and place them under the broiler. Watch and remove the sheet as soon as the layer of eggplant pieces begins to turn golden. Turn them and broil the other side the same way. From this point on you may follow the above recipe.*

110

Roasted Potato and Panir Curry

Panir made from ¾ gallon milk, cut into ¾ x ½ inch pieces, fried and soaked in boiling water [page xxi-xxii]
1 pound small new potatoes
1 tablespoon oil
½ teaspoon salt
½ teaspoon ground cumin
½ teaspoon ground coriander
½ teaspoon cayenne pepper
4 tablespoons oil
1 medium onion, finely grated
1 tablespoon fresh ginger, grated
1½ cups tomatoes, peeled and finely chopped
½ teaspoon paprika
½ teaspoon turmeric
1 teaspoon salt
3 tablespoons yogurt
2 cups water
½ teaspoon garam masala
Fresh cilantro, finely chopped, for garnish

Peel the potatoes. Cut them into halves or quarters, depending on the size, and prick them all over with a fork.

Preheat the oven to 400°. In a large bowl, mix 1 tablespoon oil, salt, cumin, coriander and red chilies. Add the potatoes to the spices and stir to coat the pieces. Place the potato pieces on a cookie sheet and roast until tender and nicely browned, stirring once or twice (30 to 45 minutes).

Heat 4 tablespoons oil on medium high. Add the onions and ginger and sauté until the onions are golden brown. Add the chopped tomatoes and cook until the oil starts to separate. Add the paprika, turmeric and salt and sauté for a couple of minutes longer. Add the yogurt, 1 tablespoon at a time, and cook until the oil begins to separate.

Stir in the potatoes, drained panir and 2 cups water. Bring to a boil. Reduce the heat to medium low and cook, covered, about 15 minutes or until the oil begins to float. Sprinkle with garam masala and garnish with cilantro.

111

Rice

Decisions about which carbohydrates to serve with a meal vary from region to region in India. In North India, most families like to have both bread and rice with their meals, while in East and South India and Kashmir, you are more likely to encounter rice than bread.

Rice is thought to be a better accompaniment with certain dals and vegetables, such as masoor dal, arhar dal, sautéed potatoes, and dry cooked green beans. Other dals and vegetables are better complemented by breads, as the menus indicate.

I prefer to serve Basmati rice, which has an appealing fragrance and visual effect. Most Indian homes will not serve Basmati rice every day, because it is a little more expensive. Here in the United States, however, it is very affordable. You may substitute long-grain rice or jasmine rice.

To prepare Basmati rice or long grain rice for cooking, wash the rice and keep rinsing until the water is clear. Soak the rice for about 20 to 30 minutes and drain it in a colander, handling the rice as little as possible. When rice has been soaked, the grains tend to break easily. To obtain perfect cooked rice, it is advisable to handle it gently and carefully. After the rice has been drained, oil and spices can be added. The butter or oil content can be decreased if desired. You may substitute brown Basmati or brown long grain rice, but you will have to experiment with regard to water content and cooking time. Brown rice absorbs more moisture and needs more cooking time.

This chapter offers recipes for rice dishes that are used repeatedly in the menus. It begins with simple recipes and goes on to include dishes such as *biryani* and *khichri*, both of which are meals in themselves.

Sada Chawal
(Plain Rice)

2 cups Basmati rice or long grain rice
1 tablespoon butter or oil
1 teaspoon salt
4 cups water

Wash and soak the rice for 20 minutes. Drain it in a fine sieve or colander.

In a heavy pot, heat the butter or oil on medium. Add the drained rice. Stir lightly until the rice grains are lightly coated with butter or oil. Add the water and bring to a vigorous boil on medium high. Reduce the heat to medium and cook, uncovered, until the water boils down to the level of the rice. Stir with a fork. Cover the pot and turn the heat to low. Simmer for 5 to 7 minutes. Stir gently with a fork again. Turn the heat off and let the rice rest for 2 to 3 minutes before serving.

Plain rice can easily be made into Zeera Rice (Cumin Rice). Add 1 teaspoon cumin seeds to the butter or oil and proceed as with Plain Rice.

Note: *Plain rice can be prepared without oil or butter. Just add rice and water and cook as the recipe requires.*

Matar Pulao
(Rice with Peas)

2 cups Basmati or long grain rice, washed, soaked and drained
3-4 tablespoons butter OR
3 tablespoons clarified butter, ghee, oil OR half-and-half mixture
of oil and ghee
2 inches stick cinnamon
2 bay leaves
2 large cardamoms OR 6 to 8 green cardamoms
6 cloves
8 peppercorns
1 medium onion, thinly sliced
10 ounces frozen peas or 1 cup of fresh shelled peas
1 teaspoon salt
4 cups water

In a large heavy pot, melt the butter or ghee on low. Stir in the spices and sauté for 30 seconds. Add the sliced onions. Turn heat to medium and sauté until the onions are golden brown.

Add the drained rice and sauté for a minute or so with the onions and spices. Raise the heat to medium high. Add the peas, salt and stir.

Add the water and turn heat to high. Bring to a boil. Cook on high until the water level is reduced to the level of the rice. Stir gently. Reduce heat to the lowest setting. Cover the pan and simmer for 5 minutes. Turn the heat off and let the rice sit for another 2 to 3 minutes before serving. Fluff the rice very gently with a fork before serving.

Tamatar Pulao
(Rice with Tomatoes)

3 to 4 tablespoons butter or vegetable oil OR
3 tablespoons of ghee
1 teaspoon cumin seeds
4 to 6 cloves
2 inch stick of cinnamon
1 large onion, finely sliced
2 cups Basmati or long grain rice, soaked for half an hour, drained and washed
3½ cups water
1 teaspoon salt or to taste
2 large or 3 medium tomatoes, thinly sliced (Peeling the tomatoes is optional.)

In a heavy pot, heat the oil, ghee or butter over medium heat. Stir in the spices and fry them for a minute. Add the onions and sauté until they are golden brown. Stir in the soaked and drained rice and stir until the rice is coated with the oil, onions and spice mixture. Add salt and water. Turn the heat to high until the uncovered pot comes to a vigorous boil.

Reduce the heat to medium and cook uncovered until half the water has evaporated, or the water levels with rice.

Gently stir the tomatoes into the rice. Turn the heat to medium low. Cover and cook until all the water has evaporated. Turn the heat off and keep the rice covered for 3 to 4 minutes or until ready to serve. Fluff with a fork before serving.

Kaju Pulao
(Rice with Cashews)

2 cups Basmati or long grain rice washed, soaked and drained
3 to 4 tablespoons butter or oil OR 3 tablespoons ghee
¾ cup raw cashews
2 bay leaves
6 cloves
6 green cardamoms
8—10 black peppercorns
2" cinnamon stick
4 cups water

In a heavy pot, heat the butter, oil or ghee on medium. Add the cashews and whole spices. Stir them for 15~20 seconds. Add the drained rice. Stir lightly until the grains of rice is lightly coated.

Add the water and bring to a vigorous boil on medium high. Reduce the heat to medium and cook until the water boils down to the level of the rice. Stir with a fork and cover the pot. Reduce the heat to low and simmer 5 to 7 minutes. Stir gently with a fork again. Turn the heat off and cover the pot. Let the rice sit for another 2 to 3 minutes before serving.

Note: If you are using roasted cashews, save them until you have reduced the heat to medium low.

Gajjar Pulao
(Rice with Carrots)

2 cups Basmati or long grain rice, washed, soaked and drained

3 to 4 tablespoons butter or oil OR 3 tablespoons ghee

1 teaspoon cumin seeds

2 or 3 bay leaves

2" cinnamon stick

1 teaspoon salt

3½ cups water

2 cups grated carrots

In a heavy pot, heat the butter, ghee or oil on medium. Add the cumin seeds and fry for 2-3 seconds. Add the remaining spices and the rice. Sauté for a couple of minutes. Add salt and water. Raise the heat to medium high and bring to a boil. Reduce the heat to medium and cook until the water boils down to the level of the rice. Stir the grated carrots into the rice. Reduce the heat to medium low. Cover the pan and cook for 5 to 7 minutes. Turn the heat off, fluff with a fork and let the rice sit, covered, for 2 to 3 minutes before serving.

Khara Masala Pulao
(Pulao with Whole Spices)

2 cups Basmati rice

3 tablespoons butter

1 teaspoon Shahi Zeera (black cumin seeds) Regular cumin seeds may be substituted.

6 cloves

6 green cardamoms, pounded

2 inch cinnamon stick

1 teaspoon salt

4 cups water

In a heavy pot, heat the butter, oil or ghee on medium. Add the whole spices. Stir them for 15~20 seconds. Add the drained rice. Stir lightly until the grains of rice are lightly coated.

Add the water and bring to a vigorous boil on medium high. Reduce the heat to medium and cook until the water boils down to the level of the rice. Stir with a fork and cover the pot. Reduce the heat to low and simmer 5 to 7 minutes. Stir gently with a fork again. Turn the heat off and cover the pot. Let the rice sit for another 2 to 3 minutes before serving.

Vegetable Biryani

1 cup of fried panir cubes, about 2", soaked in boiling water for
  30 minutes [pages xxi-xxii]
2 cups Basmati rice
4 tablespoons ghee OR 5 tablespoons butter or oil
1 teaspoon cumin seeds
6 to 8 green cardamoms
4 bay leaves
8 to 10 cloves
2" cinnamon stick
1 teaspoon black peppercorns
¾ cup raw cashews
1½ cups onions, thinly sliced
1½ tablespoons fresh ginger, minced
1 cup cauliflower, cut into 1 inch florets
1 cup peas (fresh or frozen)
¼ cup raisins
1 green chili, finely chopped
½ teaspoon cayenne pepper
2 teaspoons salt
1 cup milk
2½ cups water
1 cup carrots, grated

Soak the fried panir cubes in boiling water for 30 minutes. Wash, soak and drain the rice.

Heat the butter or ghee in a 5 -quart heavy Dutch oven on medium. Crush cumin, cardamoms, bay leaves, cloves, cinnamon, and black peppercorns; add into the pot. Sauté for a few minutes and add the cashews. Add sliced onion and ginger and sauté until golden.

Stir in the cauliflower, peas and raisins. Cook for 2 to 3 minutes, stirring gently. Add the chilies and cayenne and mix well. Add the drained rice and salt and mix well. Now add the milk and water and bring to a boil. Stir again and cook uncovered on medium until the liquid boils down to the level of the rice. Reduce the heat to low and stir in the carrots and panir cubes. Cover the pan and cook about 10 minutes. Gently fluff with a fork, turn heat off and fluff again.

Note: *If you wish to use roasted cashews, add them immediately before serving.*

Chana Dal Khichri
(Rice and Chana Dal)

1 cup chana dal
1½ cups Basmati or long grain rice
3 tablespoons oil
1 tablespoon cumin seeds
6 to 8 cloves
2 to 3 bay leaves
1 tablespoon ghee or butter
1½ cups thinly sliced onions
1½ to 2 teaspoons salt
½ teaspoon cayenne pepper
1 cup plus 2½ cups water

Wash the dal and soak it for 2 hours. Soak the rice for 20 minutes.

Heat the oil in a large, heavy Dutch oven or skillet on medium high. Add the cumin, cloves, bay leaves and ghee or butter. As soon as the ghee or butter melts, reduce the heat to medium and add the onions. Sauté the onions until they are golden brown. Remove the onions, draining the oil back into the skillet, and set aside.

Add the cayenne and washed and drained dal. Cook for 2 to 3 minutes. Add salt and 1 cup water. Bring to a boil. Reduce the heat to medium low and cook the dal for about 10 minutes. The dal should be tender but still firm.

Drain the rice and add to the dal. Add 2½ cups water. Raise the heat to medium high and bring the dal and rice to a boil. Reduce the heat to medium low and cook, covered, until all the moisture is absorbed (about 10 minutes). Turn off the heat, fluff the mixture with a fork and let it sit for a couple of minutes, covered, before serving.

Garnish with the fried onions.

Note: This dish can be served with tomato raita.

Masala Masoor Biryani
(Rice and Spicy Lentils)

This dish has three steps. Ingredients are listed separately for eachstep.

Step 1
1½" ginger root
1 clove garlic
2-3 green chilies
1 teaspoon cumin seeds
1 teaspoon fennel seeds
8-10 black peppercorns
4 cloves
1½ "cinnamon stick
4-6 green cardamoms

Grind the above into a paste, adding a little water to moisten.

1½ cups whole masoor dal
4 tablespoons cooking oil
1 onion, thinly sliced
3 tomatoes, finely chopped
1 to 2 teaspoons cayenne
¾ teaspoon turmeric
1 teaspoon salt
2 tablespoons yogurt
2 green chilies, finely chopped
1½ cups water

Wash the dal and soak it for 4-5 hours. Heat the oil and fry the thinly sliced onion until golden. Stir in the ground masala paste and cook for 4-5 minutes. Add the tomatoes and cook for about 5 to 6 minutes. Add the drained dal. Stir in the cayenne, turmeric, salt, yogurt, chilies and water. Cover and cook on low heat until the dal is tender and almost dry.

Step 2

2 cup Basmati rice, washed and soaked for ½ hour
6 cloves
10 black peppercorns
2" cinnamon stick
2 bay leaves
1 teaspoon salt
3½ cups water

Bring the water and whole spices to the boil in a 4-quart pot. Stir in the drained rice and salt and return to the boil. Reduce the heat to medium low, stir and cover. Cook the rice until the water evaporates and the rice is tender but firm. Remove the whole spices out the cooked rice, if you choose not to keep them in there before serving.

Step 3

¼ cup oil
2 onions, thinly sliced
½ cup raw cashews
5 potatoes, peeled and thinly sliced
½ teaspoon salt
1 tablespoon ghee

In a skillet, heat the oil. Add the onions and sauté until golden brown. Remove the onions and drain off the oil. Stir in the cashews and brown them in the same oil until they are pinkish in color. Drain the cashews and reserve.

Stir the potatoes into the oil. Sprinkle with salt. Cook covered for a few minutes. The potatoes should be tender but not overcooked.

In a large Dutch oven, layer the ingredients, starting with the dal mixture, followed by potatoes and rice. Repeat the layering process until all the ingredients are used, ending with rice. Drizzle the ghee over the top. Cover the Dutch oven with a damp cloth and cook, covered, for about 20 minutes on low. Garnish with cashews and fried onions.

Note: *You may substitute roasted cashews. In that case, they do not need to be fried. This biryani is a one-dish meal delicious served with mint raita.*

Khichri

Khichri is a generic name for a dish cooked with a base of rice and beans. The combination of dals can vary. This dish has rice, three dals and vegetables.

1 cup rice, washed and soaked for 1 hour
½ cup moong dal
½ cup masoor dal
¼ cup chana dal
2 tablespoons oil
1 teaspoon cumin seeds
1 or 2 dried red chilies
1 teaspoon black mustard seeds
3 cloves
1" cinnamon stick
2 to 3 bay leaves
2 teaspoons ground coriander
1 cup finely chopped onions
1 tablespoon chopped ginger
1 large potato, peeled and cut into 1/2 inch cubes
½ cup thinly sliced green beans
½ cup carrots, cut into 1/2 inch chunks
½ cup zucchini, cut into 1/2 inch chunks
¾ teaspoon turmeric
2 teaspoons salt, or to taste
8 cups water
1 cup chopped tomatoes
1 cup finely chopped spinach

Combine the dals and rice. Wash them and soak for 1 hour.

In a heavy, 5 -quart pot, heat the oil on medium high. Add the cumin seeds, chilies and mustard seeds and sauté for a few seconds. Stir in the rest of the spices and sauté for a few more seconds. Add the onion and ginger. Mix well. Reduce the heat to medium and let the onion cook, covered, for a minute or two. Uncover and stir occasionally until the onion begins to turn golden. Stir in the potatoes, beans, carrots and zucchini and cook for five minutes.

Drain the dals and rice and add to the vegetables. Stir in turmeric and salt. Mix well and bring to the boil. Reduce the heat to medium low. Cook, covered, about 20 minutes, until the rice and dals are tender. Stir in the tomatoes and spinach and simmer for another 10 to 15 minutes until the mixture begins to look like a stew.

Serve khichri with plain yogurt or raita.

Breads

In India, many different kinds of bread are prepared and enjoyed. This chapter begins with chapatis, the simple, "everyday" bread, which is cooked dry on the griddle. It offers recipes for plain parathas, which are served as a treat, and several kinds of stuffed parathas, which are very popular for special breakfasts or Sunday brunch. Stuffed parathas are normally served with yogurt, mango or apple chutney, and cucumber salad. Naan, pooris and other fried breads are reserved for special occasions.

Chapati flour is available in organic food stores or Indian grocery stores. If you cannot find it, use whole wheat pastry flour. Chapati flour is whole wheat flour and is used for making chapati, paratha or pooris.

Chapati

Chapatis

4 cups whole wheat chapati flour

1½ cups water (may take more or less quantity of water depending upon the type of flour)

½ cup ghee for brushing the chapatis (optional)

½ cup all purpose flour for dusting while rolling the chapatis

In a mixing bowl, combine the flour and water, adding the water gradually to make a smooth dough. Knead for about 10 minutes. Cover and let the dough rest for an hour. The dough should be pliable. To test, make a ball and see if it is smooth.

Preheat a skillet or griddle. Divide the dough into 20 to 24 balls. Dust each ball lightly with flour. Flatten them with the palms of your hands and roll into rounds about 4 inches in diameter. Dust again with flour on both sides. Roll into rounds about 6 to 7 inches in diameter.

Place the chapatis on the preheated griddle for a few seconds. As soon as bubbles begin to appear, turn it over and cook the other side until little brown spots begin to appear. On another burner, place a cake rack. Put the chapatis on the cake rack and keep turning it until it puffs up and light brown spots form on both sides. You may butter the top with ghee or you may leave it unbuttered.

If you want to make the chapatis in advance, it is better to butter them so that they will stay soft.

Note: *This quantity will make about 20 to 24 chapatis. You can cook as many as you need and save the dough in the refrigerator for later use. The dough will keep for three to four days.*

STEPS FOR MAKING PARATHA

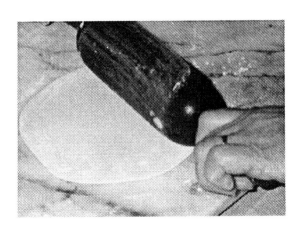

1

2

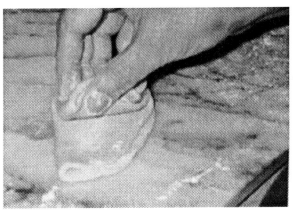

3

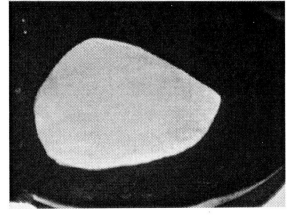

4

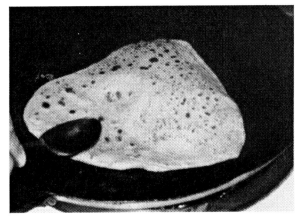

5

Paratha

4 cups whole wheat flour (preferably whole wheat pastry flouror Chapati flour)
1½ cups milk or water
½ cup oil
½ cup all purpose flour for dusting while rolling parathas

In a bowl, mix the milk or water with the flour with your hands or with the help of a pastry cutter. If necessary, add more liquid, one tablespoon at a time, to make it the consistency of bread dough. Knead the dough for at least 10 minutes. Cover the dough and let it rest for at least an hour.

Preheat an iron skillet or griddle on medium. Divide the dough into golf ball-sized balls. Dust each ball lightly with flour. Flatten them with the palms of your hands and roll them into 4-inch rounds. Brush each round with oil. Fold in half and brush with oil again. Fold again to make a triangle. Dust with flour and roll the triangle to about 6-7 inches.

Place a paratha on the preheated griddle for 5 to 7 seconds. Turn over, brush with oil and turn over again. Brush the second side with oil. Cook until both sides have golden brown spots. The surface should be lightly crispy. Remove the paratha from the griddle. Place on a paper towel to absorb the excess oil.

This recipe will make about 20 parathas.

Note: *Parathas taste best when they are hot off the griddle, but you may cook them in advance. Wrap them in foil and reheat at 200° for about 30 minutes.*

Cauliflower Paratha

2 cups whole wheat flour
¾ cup water
½ cup flour for dusting

In a mixing bowl, combine the flour and water, mixing them together with your hands or with the help of a stand mixer. If necessary, add more water, one tablespoon at a time, until the dough is the consistency of bread dough.

Knead for 5 to 7 minutes. Cover the dough and let it rest for at least an hour.

For filling:
2 cups grated cauliflower
1/4 cup onions, finely chopped
2 tablespoons cilantro, chopped
1 tablespoon ginger, minced
1 or 2 green chilies, finely chopped
1 teaspoon garam masala
1 teaspoon amchur (*optional*)
1 teaspoon salt
1/2 cup oil for frying

Mix all the ingredients except salt and oil. Preheat an oiled griddle on medium high.

Stuffing cauliflower parathas is a little complicated. You may use the technique described for potato parathas, but there is another technique that may be a bit easier. Divide the dough into 20 to 22 small balls. Roll out two balls to make discs 3 or 4 inches in diameter. Place 1½ to 2 tablespoons of the cauliflower mixture on one disc. Sprinkle a little salt over the filling.

Cover with the second disc and press the edges together. The paratha should be sealed on all sides. Pick up this stuffed paratha and dust it with flour and roll it again gently so that it is about 6 to 7 inches in diameter. (If you mix the salt in the filling, it will become too moist to roll. It is better to sprinkle a little salt on each paratha fillings.)

Santosh Jain

Reduce the heat to medium. Place the paratha on the preheated griddle. As soon as the bottom side shows some tan spots, turn it over and spread a little oil on the cooked side. Turn again and spread a little oil on the second side. Turn the paratha a couple of times without adding any oil. With a spatula, gently flatten the paratha in a circular motion while frying. The paratha should be a little crisp.

Serve hot with chutney and yogurt.

Note: *If you wish to make all of the parathas at once, you may pile them up, wrap in foil and keep them warm for a while in a 200° oven.*

Dill Paratha

1½ cups whole wheat flour
¾ cup gram flour
¾ to 1 teaspoon salt
1 teaspoon ajwain
2 tablespoons yogurt
1½ cups chopped fresh dill
1/4 cup fined chopped onions or scallions
1 or 2 finely chopped green chilies
½ to ¾ cup of water
Flour for dusting
About ½ cup oil for frying

In a large bowl, mix the two flours, salt, ajwain and yogurt with your fingers. Add dill, onions or scallions and green chilies. Add water a little at a time and mix the dough until the ingredients are thoroughly combined. The dough should be a little thicker than bread dough. Knead the dough for 5 to 7 minutes. Let it rest covered for about 20 minutes.

Divide the dough into 12 to 14 portions and roll into balls. Dust one ball with flour so that all sides are covered with flour. Now roll it into a 4 to 5 inch round. Brush it with a little oil; fold it in half and half again until it forms a triangle. Dust the triangle in flour and roll again. You may need to dust again. The finished paratha should be about 6 to 7 inches in diameter.

Preheat a griddle on medium high. Brush a little oil on the griddle. Place the paratha on the preheated griddle. As soon as the bottom side shows some pink-brown spots, turn the paratha and spread a little oil over the top. Keep turning so that both sides cook evenly. Oil each side only once. Press down the paratha gently with a spatula.

The parathas should be a little crispy and should look like cooked pancakes. Serve hot with chutney and yogurt.

Note: *If you wish to make all of the parathas at once, you may wrap them in foil and keep them warm for a while in a 200° oven.*

Moong Dal Paratha

1 cup split moong dal (with skins)
1 inch piece fresh ginger, coarsely chopped
2 green chilies, coarsely chopped
1 large potato, boiled and peeled
1 cup greens (fresh spinach, watercress or tender leaves of radishes), finely chopped
½ cup finely chopped onion
½ cup yogurt
1½ teaspoons salt
3 cups whole wheat flour
Oil for frying

Soak the dal for two hours. Drain well. Add the ginger and chilies and grind coarsely in the food processor. You may need to add 1 or 2 tablespoons water.

Grate the boiled potato. In a large bowl, combine the potato with greens, onion, yogurt, and salt. Add the ground dal mixture and mix well. Add the flour. Mix and knead to form a dough. The dough may be a little sticky.

Divide the dough into 20 portions and roll into balls. Dust one ball with flour so that all sides are covered with flour. Now roll it into a 4 to 5 inch round. Brush it with a little oil; fold it in half and half again until it forms a triangle. Dust the triangle in flour and roll again. You may need to dust again. The finished paratha should be about 6 to 7 inches in diameter.

Preheat a griddle on medium high. Brush a little oil on the griddle. Place the paratha on the preheated griddle. As soon as the bottom side shows some pink-brown spots, turn the paratha and spread a little oil over the top. Keep turning so that both sides cook evenly. Oil each side only once. Press down the paratha gently with a spatula.

The parathas should be a little crispy and should look like cooked pancakes. Serve hot with chutney and yogurt.

Note: *If you wish to make all of the parathas at once, you may wrap them in foil and keep them warm for a while in a 200° oven.*

Potato Paratha

2 cups whole wheat flour
3/4 cup water
½ cup extra flour for dusting
½ cup oil for frying

In a mixing bowl, combine the flour and water, mixing them together with your hands or with the help of a stand mixer. If necessary, add more water, one tablespoon at a time, until the dough is the consistency of chapati dough.
Knead for 5 to 7 minutes. Let the dough sit covered for at least an hour.

For potato filling:

1 pound boiled potatoes
½ cup fined chopped onions or scallions
1 tablespoon finely chopped green chilies (optional)
2 tablespoons finely chopped cilantro
¾ teaspoon garam masala
½ teaspoon ajwain
1 teaspoon salt
1 teaspoon crushed dry mint
1 teaspoon amchur (optional)

Cool the potatoes. Peel and mash them. Add the remaining filling ingredients and mix well.

Assembling the parathas:

Divide the dough into 10 to 12 portions. Dust with flour and roll so that all sides are covered with flour. Now roll the ball into a 4 to 5 inch disc. Place the lump of potato filling right in the middle of the disc. Fold the dough over the filling and pinch the edges together to enclose the filling. Flatten the filled paratha. Dust with flour and roll it gently to make a round, turning it over once or twice during rolling. You should have a round about 6 to 7 inches in diameter.

Santosh Jain

Cooking the parathas:

Preheat an oiled griddle on medium high. Place the paratha on the griddle. As soon as the bottom side shows some tan spots, turn it over and spread a little oil on the cooked side. Turn again and spread a little oil on the second side. Turn the paratha a couple of times without adding any oil. With a spatula, gently press the paratha in a circular motion. The paratha should be a little crispy. Serve hot with chutney and yogurt.

Note: *If you wish to make all of the parathas at once, you may pile them up, wrap in foil and keep them warm for a while in a 200° oven.*

Naan

1 teaspoon yeast
¼ cup warm water
4 cups all purpose flour
1 teaspoon sugar
3 tablespoons vegetable oil
1 teaspoon salt
2 tablespoons yogurt
½ cup warm milk
½ - ¾ cup warm water
1 tablespoon yogurt
2 tablespoons water

Dissolve the yeast in ¼ cup of warm water. In a large bowl, mix flour, sugar, oil, salt and yogurt. Mix well. Stir in the warm milk and yeast. Add the remaining ½ to ¾ cup of water as needed to produce dough similar to the consistency of bread dough. Knead the dough until it is smooth, about 10 minutes.

Form the dough into a ball and place it in a lightly oiled bowl. Turn it once to coat the surface of the dough with oil. Cover with a cloth and let it rise in a warm place for 2 to 2½ hrs.

Pre—heat the broiler.

Punch down the dough and let it rest for 10 minutes. Pinch off golf ball-sized pieces of dough and roll them into balls. Let them rise for another 10 minutes. Dust the balls with flour and roll each ball into an oval about 6 inches long and ¼ inch thick.

Mix 1 tablespoon yogurt with 2 tablespoons water. Brush each naan with the mixture. Place three or four naans on an oiled baking sheet. Place the rack so that the naans are about 6 to 8 inches from the broiler. Broil, watching carefully; the tops will be done in 2 to 3 minutes. Turn the naans and broil the other side. They should puff up and have gold spots all over the top.

Serve hot.

Santosh Jain

Note: *To save time you may divide the dough into four large balls. Roll them and place them on an oiled pizza tray and broil them as smaller naans. Cut them into small pieces before serving.*

Naan with Onions

1 teaspoon dry yeast
¼ cup warm water
4 cups all-purpose flour
3 tablespoons oil
1 teaspoon sugar
1 teaspoon salt
2 tablespoons yogurt
½ cup warm milk
2 tablespoons dehydrated onions
½ - ¾ cup warm water
1 tablespoon yogurt
2 tablespoons water

Dissolve yeast in 1/4 cup warm water. In a large bowl, combine flour, sugar, oil, salt and yogurt. Mix well.

Stir in the warm milk and yeast. Add the onions. Gradually add the remaining ½-¾ cup water to form a dough the consistency of bread dough. Knead well until smooth.

Form the dough into a ball and place it in a lightly oiled bowl. Turn it once to coat the surface of the dough with oil. Cover with a cloth and let it rise in a warm place for 2 to 2½ hrs.

Pre—heat the broiler and set the rack 6 to 8 inches below the grill. Punch down the dough and let it rest for 10 minutes. Divide the dough into golf-ball-size balls. Let rest for another 10 minutes. Dust them with flour and roll them into ovals about 6" long and ¼" thick.

Mix the 1 tablespoon yogurt with 2 tablespoons water. Place three to four naans on an oiled baking sheet; brush the naans with yogurt and broil. Watch carefully; the top will be done in 2 to 3 minutes. Turn the naans and broil the second side. They should have gold spots all over the puff up. Serve hot.

Alu Naan
(Potato-stuffed Naan)

1 package yeast
¼ cup warm water
4 cups all purpose flour
1 teaspoon sugar
3 tablespoons vegetable oil
1 teaspoon salt
2 tablespoons yogurt
½ cup warm milk
½ - ¾ cup warm water
1 tablespoon yogurt
2 tablespoons water

For filling:
2 large boiled potatoes, grated
1green chili, minced, or 1/2 teaspoon cayenne pepper
2 tablespoons cilantro, finely chopped
½ teaspoon garam masala
½ teaspoon ajwain
½ teaspoon salt

Mix all the spice and herbs with the potatoes.

For naan:

Dissolve the yeast in ¼ cup of warm water. In a large bowl, thoroughly mix flour, sugar, oil, salt and yogurt. Stir in the warm milk and yeast. Add the remaining ½ to ¾ cup of water as needed to produce a dough the consistency of bread dough. Knead the dough until it is smooth, about 10 minutes.

Form the dough into a ball and place it in a lightly oiled bowl. Turn it once to coat the surface of the dough with oil. Cover with a cloth and let it rise in a warm place for 2 to 2 ½ hours.

Pre—heat the broiler.

Punch down the dough and let it rest for 10 minutes. Pinch off golfball-sized pieces of dough and roll them into balls. Dust the balls with floor and roll each ball into a five inch disk.

Put a tablespoon of filling in the middle of a disk. Pinch the ends to enclose the fillings so that the filling does not show. Repeat until all the naans have been filled. Let stuffed balls sit for another 10 minutes. Roll each ball into 7 to 8 inch disk.

Mix 1 tablespoon yogurt with 2 tablespoons water. Brush each naan with the mixture. Place three or four naans on an oiled baking sheet. Place the rack so that the naans are about 6 to 8 inches from the broiler. Broil, watching carefully; the tops will be done in 2 to 3 minutes. Turn the naans and broil the other side. They should puff up and have gold spots all over the top.

Serve hot.

Panir Naan
(Panir-stuffed Naan)

1 package yeast
¼ cup warm water
4 cups all purpose flour
1 teaspoon sugar
3 tablespoons vegetable oil
1 teaspoon salt
2 tablespoons yogurt
½ cup warm milk
½ -¾ cup warm water
1 tablespoon yogurt
2 tablespoons water

For filling:

2 cups crumbled panir
1green chili, minced, or ½ teaspoon cayenne pepper
2 tablespoons cilantro, finely chopped
½ teaspoon garam masala
½ teaspoon ground coriander
½ teaspoon ground cumin
½ teaspoon salt

Mix all the spices and herbs into the panir.

For panir naan:

Pre—heat the broiler.

Dissolve the yeast in 1/4 cup of warm water. In a large bowl, thoroughly mix flour, sugar, oil, salt and yogurt. Stir in the warm milk and yeast. Add the remaining ½ to ¾ cup of water as needed to produce a dough the consistency of bread dough. Knead the dough until it is smooth, about 10 minutes.

Form the dough into a ball and place it in a lightly oiled bowl. Turn it once to coat the surface of the dough with oil. Cover with a cloth and let it rise in a warm place for 2 to 2 ½ hours. Punch down the dough and let it rest for 10 minutes. Pinch off golfball-sized pieces of dough and roll them into balls. Dust the balls with floor and roll each ball into a five inch disk.

Put a tablespoon of filling in the middle of a disk. Pinch the ends to enclose the filling so that the filling does not show. Repeat until all the balls have been filled. Let the stuffed balls rest for another 10 minutes. Roll each ball into a 7 to 8 inch disk.

Mix 1 tablespoon yogurt with 2 tablespoons water. Brush each naan with the mixture. Place three or four naans on an oiled baking sheet. Place the rack so that the naans are about 6 to 8 inches from the broiler. Broil, watching carefully; the tops will be done in 2 to 3 minutes.

Turn the naans and broil the other side. They should puff up and have gold spots all over the top.

Serve hot.

Alu Kulcha
(Baked Flat Bread Stuffed with Potatoes)

3 cups white flour
1 cup semolina
3 tablespoons potato flour
¾ cup yogurt
1 teaspoon salt
1 tablespoon yeast
1 teaspoon sugar
2 tablespoons vegetable oil
1 cup hot water
2 large boiled potatoes
2 tablespoons cilantro, minced
½ green chili, minced
½ teaspoon garam masala
½ teaspoon ajwain
½ teaspoon salt
1 tablespoon yogurt in two tablespoons water
4 tablespoons melted butter

In a large bowl mix semolina, potato flour, salt, yeast and sugar. Add oil and yogurt and mix well. Add the hot water gradually. You may use all the water or a little less or a little more, depending on the weather, etc. The mixture should be soft. Knead well, put in an oiled bowl, turn to oil the top and let the dough rest for 2½ to 3 hours.

Grate the boiled potatoes and mix with the cilantro, chili, garam masala, ajwain and salt. Set aside.

Make golfball-sized balls out of the dough. You should have about 22 to 25 balls. Flatten each ball in your hands to about 4 inches diameter.

Place a tablespoon of stuffing in the middle of a round. Pinch all the edges into the middle so that all the stuffing is enclosed. Continue until all rounds are stuffed. Let the stuffed balls sit for 10 minutes.

Preheat the over to 500° F. Dust each ball with flour and roll into a disc about 6 to 7 inches in diameter.

Mix yogurt with water. Brush with yogurt and water mixture. Place the discs on a cookie sheet or pizza tray. (You might be able to place 4 to 5 discs on the cookie sheet.) Bake for about 10-15 minutes or until pink dots show up on the top and the bottom is also baked. Brush them with melted butter (optional).

Fold them in a thick towel in a bread basket. Repeat the process until all are cooked. Serve them while they are still warm.

Poodina Kulcha
(Mint Bread)

1 tablespoon dry yeast
¼ cup warm water
4 cups white flour
½ teaspoon baking soda
1 teaspoon salt
1 teaspoon sugar
2 tablespoons oil
3 tablespoons yogurt
1¼ cups warm milk

Filling:
1 cup mint finely chopped
½ teaspoon ajwain
1 teaspoon salt
1 large red onion, finely chopped
½ cup cilantro, finely chopped

Dissolve yeast in warm water. Mix the flour, baking soda, salt and sugar. Add the yogurt and mix lightly. Add the oil and dissolved yeast and knead with warm milk. Add the milk slowly. The dough should neither be too soft or too stiff.

Brush the dough with oil and put it in a plastic bag large enough to allow the dough to rise. Cover the dough with a large bowl, inverted, and let it sit for 2½ to 3 hours. Punch down and let it rise again for 30 minutes.

Mix all the filling ingredients together.

Preheat the oven to 500 degrees and keep a large greased cookie sheet in the oven.

Divide the dough into golfball-sized pieces. Roll each piece into a 6" or 7" disk. Sprinkle one portion of filling on the rolled bread disks and press it gently with your fingers. Put four or five pieces in the oven and bake until the bottoms turn golden brown and the tops are lightly browned.

Poori

4 cup whole wheat pastry flour
2 tablespoon oil
1 teaspoon salt
1¼ cups water plus additional if needed
1 teaspoon ajwain or carom seeds (optional)
Approximately 3 cups oil for deep frying

Combine flour, oil and salt in a large bowl. Add the water slowly and form the mixture into a dough. Knead for at least 10 minutes. The dough should have a smooth consistency. It should be a little stiffer than the dough for chapatis. Let the dough rest for about half an hour.

Divide the dough into balls a little smaller than golfballs. Use a little oil to moisten your hands, the rolling pin and the board. Flatten each ball into a disc and roll it evenly into a round 4 to 5 inches in diameter.

Heat the oil to smoking in the wok or skillet. Reduce the heat to medium high. Gently slide one poori into the hot oil. It will start to puff up after a few seconds. Turn it over gently a few times till you get pinkish color. Remove with a slotted spoon, draining off as much oil as possible by holding the poori on the spoon against the side of the wok. Continue until all the pooris have been cooked. Place the cooked pooris in a bowl lined with paper towels.

If you are making pooris alone, roll them all out and place them on a cookie sheet. You can stack them if you place a dish towel between the layers. If you have a partner, one person can roll out the pooris while the other fries them.

Pooris should be served hot. Ideally, each poori should be served immediately after it is fried. However, they can be kept hot in a 200° oven with the door slightly ajar. Plan the meal so that frying the pooris is the last thing you do before sitting down to eat.

Note: *Be sure that the oil is really hot. To test it, drop a little piece of dough in the oil. If it floats immediately, the oil is hot enough.*

147

Methi Poori
(Poori with Fenugreek)

3 cups whole wheat flour
1 cup gram flour (chickpea flour)
½ teaspoon salt
½ teaspoon cayenne
1 tablespoon oil
¾ cup cooked spinach, finely chopped
1 tablespoon crushed dry fenugreek leaves
1 cup water
Approximately 3 cups oil for deep frying

Mix the flours with the salt, cayenne and oil. Add the spinach and fenugreek leaves and mix the dough with your fingers. Add the water gradually. Knead the dough until it is smooth. The dough should be a little stiffer than chapati dough. Put the dough in an oiled bowl and turn it to cover the surface with oil. Cover the bowl and let the dough rest for 20 minutes. If you are going to fry the pooris later, refrigerate the dough.

Divide the dough into balls a little smaller than golfballs. You will have about 30 pieces. Oil your palms and roll each piece into a ball. With a rolling pin, roll each ball into a 4-5 inch round.

Heat the oil for frying on high. When the oil is hot, slide one poori into the oil and press it down gently with a spatula or slotted spoon. It should puff up quickly. Turn again and cook until both sides are light golden brown.

Remove with a slotted spoon, draining off as much oil as possible by holding the poori on the spoon against the side of the wok. Continue until all the pooris have been cooked. Place the cooked pooris in a bowl lined with paper towels.

Kashmiri Poori
(Whole Wheat Leavened Fried Bread)

1 tablespoon dry yeast
2 tablespoons warm water
3 cups whole wheat pastry or chapati flour
1 cup unbleached flour
1 teaspoon sugar
½ teaspoon salt
1 teaspoon baking powder
½ teaspoon lightly crushed fennel seed
3 tablespoons yogurt
¾ cup warm milk
1 tablespoon ghee or oil
½ cup warm water
Oil for deep frying

Dissolve the yeast in 2 tablespoons water and let it sit for 5 minutes.

In a large bowl, mix the flours, sugar, salt, baking powder and fennel seed. Add the yeast, yogurt and warm milk and ghee. Mix well. The dough will be coarse, resembling pastry dough. Add the warm water gradually and knead the dough. The dough should be pliable. Cover the dough and let it rest for 2 to 3 hours.

Grease your hands and form the dough into 25 or 30 a little smaller than golfball-sized balls. Heat the oil in a wok or pan on medium high. To test the temperature of the oil, drop in a small ball of dough. If it rises, sizzling, immediately, the oil is ready.

Roll each ball into a 4-5 inch round. Slide one round down the side of the wok into the oil. As soon as it begins to puff, turn it and gently press it down into the hot oil. Turn again and fry until both sides are light golden brown. Drain on paper towels. Repeat until all the pooris are fried. Serve hot.

Bhaturas

1½ cups semolina
½ cup water
1 package dry yeast
¼ cup warm water
3 cups flour
2 tablespoons yogurt
¾ cup hot water
½ teaspoon salt
½ teaspoon sugar
Approximately 3 cups vegetable oil for deep frying

Soak the semolina in ½ cup water for two hours.

Make the dough for the bhaturas about 3 hours before you fry them. Dissolve the yeast in 1/4 cup warm water. Place the soaked semolina in a large mixing bowl and add the flour, yogurt, salt and sugar. Stir in the yeast and mix well. Add the hot water gradually and knead the dough until it is smooth. You may not need to add all of the water. The dough should be the consistency of pizza dough. If it is too dry, add water, 1 tablespoon at a time, until it reaches the desired consistency. Brush the dough with a little oil and let it rest, covered, for three hours.

Oil your hands and divide the dough into 25 balls about the size of a little smaller than golf balls. Cover with a dish towel and let them rest for about 10 minutes.

Lightly oil a rolling pin and roll each ball into a 5 inch round. As you roll out the bhaturas, heat the oil for deep frying in a wok or deep skillet until it is smoking. Reduce the heat to medium high. Slide each bhatura gently into the hot oil. As they cook, they will float to the top and puff up. Turn them gently to cook on the other side until all sides are light golden.

Do not be too concerned if each bhatura does not puff up. If properly cooked, they will taste just as good.

Raita

Dahi or yogurt is made daily in almost every household and served with almost every meal. Its cooling quality complements spicy foods. Many Indian meals are served with plain yogurt, which is usually homemade, but a variety of vegetables and fruits may be added to the yogurt to make delicious raitas.

Once you get the hang of it, yogurt is quite easy to make. Use 2 percent milk for yogurt, rather than skim milk. Skim milk produces a thin, watery yogurt that is not desirable. I prefer to use Erivan acidophilus yogurt, which contains no gluten; it is available at health food stores. If Erivan is not available, plain (unflavored) Dannon yogurt works quite well.

To make yogurt, boil 1 quart milk in a 3-quart saucepan or in the microwave. It takes about 10-12 minutes to boil a quart of milk in the microwave. When the milk has reached a full boil, remove it from the heat and let it cool down until it is comfortable to the touch. The temperature should be 90-95° F in the winter or 80-85° F in the summer.

Put 2 tablespoons yogurt in a glass jar or glass or pyrex bowl. Smear the yogurt over the bottom and sides of the jar. Pour the boiled milk into the jar and stir well. Cover the jar and wrap it with a small blanket or heavy towel. In the summer, let it sit on the counter. It should take eight to ten hours; letting it sit overnight works well. Refrigerate until needed.

Some recipes call for sour yogurt. To sour the yogurt, let it sit at room temperature for an additional 24 hours.

The following recipes for raitas use homemade yogurt. If you wish to use commercial yogurt, you may do so. In that case you may have to thin it a little by adding some water.

151

Mint Raita

Yogurt made from 1 quart milk
1 teaspoon salt
2 tablespoons fresh mint, minced, OR 1 tablespoon crushed dried mint
1 teaspoon whole cumin seeds, dry roasted and ground
Freshly ground black pepper to taste

In a deep bowl, stir the yogurt until smooth. Stir in the salt and mix well. Add the mint and blend it with the yogurt. Sprinkle cumin and black pepper on top. Refrigerate and serve cold.

Potato Raita

Yogurt made from 1 quart milk
Salt and freshly ground black pepper to taste
3 medium boiling potatoes, boiled and peeled; and cut into small cubes
½ teaspoon crushed dry mint leaves
Paprika for garnish

Stir the yogurt until smooth. Stir in the salt and pepper and add the potatoes. Mix gently. Garnish with the mint leaves and sprinkle with paprika just before serving.

Spinach Raita

Yogurt made from 1 quart milk
1 pound fresh spinach
1 teaspoon salt
Freshly ground pepper to taste
1 teaspoon oil
1 teaspoon black mustard seeds
½ teaspoon paprika or cayenne pepper

Wash the spinach thoroughly in cold water and drain it in a colander. Chop the spinach finely and steam until it is barely tender. Remove and plunge in ice cold water. Drain thoroughly. Squeeze the spinach between your hands to remove as much water as possible.

Stir the yogurt until it is smooth. Add the salt and mix thoroughly. Stir in the spinach.

Heat the oil in a small skillet. When the oil is hot, add the mustard seeds. Cover the pan and remove from the heat. Wait until seeds stop popping. Add the seeds to the raita and mix gently. Sprinkle the raita with little paprika or cayenne for garnish.

Refrigerate and serve cold.

Zucchini Raita

Yogurt made from 1 quart milk
1 pound zucchini
1 teaspoon salt
Freshly ground black pepper
1 teaspoon whole cumin seeds, dry roasted and ground Paprika

Scrub the zucchini. If it is fresh and tender, do not peel it. Coarsely grate the zucchini and steam cook for about 3 minutes. Plunge into ice cold water. Drain thoroughly. Press the zucchini between your hands, squeezing out as much water as possible.

Stir the yogurt until smooth. Add salt and mix well. Stir in the zucchini.

Sprinkle pepper, cumin and paprika on top. Refrigerate and serve cold.

Tomato Raita

Dahi (yogurt) made from 1 quart milk
2 cups tomatoes (preferably plum tomatoes), chopped
Salt to taste
Freshly ground pepper
1 teaspoon whole cumin seeds, dry roasted and ground
2 tablespoons cilantro, finely chopped, for garnish

In a deep bowl, beat the yogurt until smooth. Stir in the salt and pepper and add the chopped tomatoes. Sprinkle the top with the cumin seeds and garnish with cilantro.

Cucumber Raita

1 quart yogurt
2 cups cucumbers, peeled, grated and squeezed
Salt and freshly ground pepper to taste
1 teaspoon whole cumin seeds, dry roasted and ground
2 tablespoons cilantro, finely chopped, for garnish

Mix the yogurt with the grated cucumbers. Stir in the salt and pepper and garnish with cumin seeds and cilantro.

Note: *If you are using tender European cucumbers, you don't need to peel them.*

Sweet Onion and Mint Raita

Follow the mint raita recipe, but add 1 cup finely chopped sweet onion.

Note: *If you soak the chopped onion in ice water for half an hour before adding them to the yogurt, they will be crisp.*

Boondi Ka Raita (Raita with Little Gram Flour Dumplings)

½ cup gram flour
¼ teaspoon freshly ground black pepper
6 tablespoons water
Oil for deep frying
4 hot cups water
1 teaspoon salt
Yogurt made from 1 quart milk
½ teaspoon crushed roasted cumin
A sprinkle of cayenne or paprika
Freshly ground black pepper
Strainer with big wholes

In a bowl, combine the gram flour and pepper. Adding the water slowly, beat with a fork until the batter is the consistency of mustard.

In a heavy pan or wok, heat the oil on medium. Holding a strainer over the pan, spoon the batter through the strainer and into the hot oil. Small drops of the batter will drop into the oil. As soon as they begin floating to the top, remove them with a slotted spoon. Repeat until all the batter has been used up.

Put the hot water and salt in a bowl. Soak the boondi for 10 minutes. Drain the boondi and gently squeeze out the water with your hands. Cool.

In a serving bowl, beat the yogurt smooth and season with salt and freshly ground black pepper to taste. Stir in the boondi.

Sprinkle with roasted cumin and paprika or cayenne and serve.

Note: *You will need a strainer with ¼ inch size holes. You may try using the wrong side of a flat grater with ¼ inch holes.*

Moong Pakori Raita

¾ cup washed moong dal, soaked in cold water overnight
1½-inch piece of fresh ginger
½ teaspoon garam masala
Oil for deep frying
Yogurt made from 1 quart milk
Salt and pepper to taste
Pinch of paprika or cayenne
1 teaspoon cumin seeds, dry roasted and ground

Rub the soaked dal between your hands, draining the dal and adding fresh water and draining again.

Scrape the ginger and chop finely. Put the ginger in a blender and add 4 tablespoons water and 4 tablespoons dal. Grind to a thick paste. Remove the ground dal and add more, a little at a time, using as little water as possible. The paste should be thick but a little grainy.

Add the garam masala and whip the dal paste until it is light and fluffy. To test, drop a little dal into a bowl of water; it should be light enough to float.

In a wok or deep skillet, heat the oil on medium high. Dip your fingers into the paste and gently drop small quantities of the paste into the hot oil. Remove the little balls as they turn a light golden color. Soak them in salted hot water for 30 minutes.

Beat the yogurt until smooth, seasoning to taste with salt and black pepper.

Remove the soaked pakoras from the hot water and press them gently between your hands to extract all the water. Stir them into the beaten yogurt.

Garnish with cayenne and roasted cumin.

Note: *If you experience difficulty in making pakoras with your fingers, you may use a wet teaspoon for dropping the pakoras into the oil.*

Apple Raita

Dahi (yogurt) made from 1 quart milk
2 cups Granny Smith apples, grated
Salt to taste
Freshly ground black pepper
1 teaspoon whole cumin seeds, dry roasted and crushed

In a deep bowl, beat the yogurt until smooth. Stir in salt. Add the apples and blend into the yogurt.

Sprinkle freshly ground pepper and crushed cumin on top. Refrigerate and serve cold.

Desserts

Desserts are not an essential part of Indian meals; they are usually reserved for special occasions. To satisfy a sweet tooth, people may finish a meal with a piece of fresh fruit in season, sometimes with a little yogurt sweetened with sugar.

Sometimes desserts like *gulab jamun* may be served at tea time. When visitors drop by, sweets may be offered with savory snacks. Halwa and kheer are important in Hindu mythology and are often served for religious special occasions.

Jalebi
(Sweet, Crispy & Soft Pretzels)

1 teaspoon dry yeast
½ cup plus 4 tablespoons warm water
1 cup all-purpose flour
1 tablespoon gram flour
1½ cups sugar
¾ cup water
1 inch cinnamon stick
2-3 cups oil for deep frying.

Soak the yeast in warm water for 5 minutes. Add remaining ingredients and beat well to make a smooth batter. If necessary, add 3 to 4 tablespoons water. The batter should be slightly thicker than beaten egg.

To make the syrup, combine sugar with 3/4 cups water and cinnamon stick in a medium—sized pot and cook on high until water comes to a boil. Reduce the heat to low and simmer for about 5 minutes.

In a deep skillet, heat the oil on medium. Fill a pastry bag about three-quarters full with the batter. Squeeze the batter into the hot oil with a circular motion, forming pretzel—like shapes. With a pair of tongs, turn each piece as soon as it becomes a light golden color. Dip in the hot syrup and remove immediately. Jalebis should be crisp. If they are soggy, the syrup needs to be cooked to a thicker consistency.

Note: *You can use a Rubbermaid catsup dispenser bottle instead of a pastry bag.*

Try the crispness of the jalebi by frying one and after soaking in the syrup. If the jalebi is soggy, it means that the syrup needs to be cooked a little longer to get the desired crispness.

Suji Halwa
(Cream of Wheat Halwa)

8 green cardamoms
8 cups water
2 cups sugar
1" cinnamon stick
8 ounces unsalted butter
2 cups Cream of Wheat
2 ounces golden raisins
2 ounces slivered almonds

Pound the cardamoms and separate the shells from the seeds. Mix water, sugar, cinnamon stick and cardamom shells in a 4-quart pot and bring to a boil. Turn the heat to low and simmer for 5 minutes.

Melt the butter in a large heavy skillet on medium. Add the Cream of Wheat and cardamom seeds and cook, stirring constantly. If the mixture is not stirred carefully, the Cream of Wheat will burn. When it starts to turn pink and butter begins to separate a little, add the raisins. After the raisins puff up, gently stir in the sugar syrup and continue stirring until the water evaporates. Turn the heat off and cover the skillet for a few minutes.

Garnish with almonds and serve hot.

Note: *As soon as you add the syrup, stir and cover quickly because the halwa will start to splatter.*

Carrot Halwa

Panir made from 1 quart milk
1 quart half and half
6 ounces unsalted butter
3 pounds carrots, peeled and coarsely grated
2 cups sugar
½ cup golden raisins
¾ cup sliced almonds
12 cardamoms
Pistachios and almonds for garnish.

Pour the half and half into a heavy saucepan (preferably nonstick) and heat on high. Stir and watch carefully so that the cream does not boil over. If the liquid rises too high, remove the pan from the heat. As soon as the liquid goes down again, return the pan to the heat. Stir constantly. The liquid should reduce to about half the original quantity and should thicken to a consistency somewhat thicker than heavy cream.

Crumble the panir with your fingers and add to the cooked half and half, stirring and mixing over medium heat for about 5 minutes. This is *Khoya*.

Put the carrots and 2 cups sugar into a heavy base non stick skillet. Cook on medium high for about 30 minutes. You will not need to stir very often once the mixture begins to give off moisture. The goal is to dry out the carrots without overcooking.

Stir in 6 ounces butter in the carrots and stir fry them on medium low heat. Stir constantly until the butter begins to shine on the carrots, about 10 minutes. Add raisins, almonds and crushed cardamom seeds.

Add *khoya* to the carrots and gently mix it while keeping it on medium low heat for about 10 minutes. Turn off the heat. Mix thoroughly. Reheat before serving and garnish with pistachios and almonds.

Note: *Carrot halwa can be refrigerated or frozen. It should be served warm.*

Raj Bhog Halwa
(Royal Halwa)

1 cup gram flour
1 cup suji or cream of wheat
8 ounces unsalted butter
1 cup khoya (See the recipe in "Techniques" [page11])
½ cup golden raisins (optional)
½ cup slivered blanched almonds
½ cup raw broken cashews
¼ cup chopped unsalted pistachios
1 tablespoon cardamom seeds
A pinch of saffron or ½ teaspoon yellow food coloring
2 cups sugar
4 cups water

Melt the butter in a large heavy skillet on medium heat. Add the suji and cardamom seeds and sauté for 3—4 minutes. Add gram flour and continue to sauté until the color starts to turn to pink and the melted butter starts to separate. This step may take 30 to 40 minutes.

Crumble the khoya and add it to the suji and gram flour mixture and sauté again for about 7 to 8 minutes or until the butter starts to separate. Add half the almonds, cashews and raisins. Stir for a couple of minutes. The cashews will brown a little, and the raisins will puff up a little.

In the meantime, make syrup with sugar and water. Bring to a boil then add crushed saffron or food coloring. Cook the mixture for a couple of minutes. Gently stir the syrup into the mixture (halwa). Cover and let it cook for couple of minutes. Turn the heat off. Let it sit for about five minutes. Fluff the halwa with a fork and garnish with the rest of the almonds and chopped pistachios.

Halwa is always served warm. It can be refrigerated or frozen and reheated before serving.

STEPS FOR MAKING GULAB JAMUN

1

2

3

4

Gulab Jamun

2½ cups sugar
3 cups water
Panir prepared from 1 quart milk
2 cups Carnation powdered milk
6 tablespoons all-purpose flour
2 heaping tablespoons solidified ghee.
1-2 teaspoons crushed cardamom seeds
Pinch of baking soda
½ cup milk

To make the syrup, combine sugar and water in a saucepan and cook on high until the water comes to a boil. Reduce the heat to medium and cook for a total of 10 to 15 minutes. Keep the syrup hot but not cooking.

To make the Gulab Jamun, crumble the panir in a large mixing bowl and add powdered milk, flour, ghee, crushed cardamoms, and baking soda. Mix thoroughly. Add the milk slowly and knead the mixture into a dough. The dough should be soft and smooth enough to shape into balls without cracking. Roll and shape into 32 walnut—size balls.

Heat the oil in a wok or skillet on medium heat. The oil should not be so hot that it begins to smoke. Test it by dropping a small bit of dough into the oil. If the oil is ready, the dough will float to the surface immediately without browning. Drop the balls into the hot oil a few at a time. Keep turning them gently to brown them slowly and evenly on all sides. When they are dark brown, remove them and drain off as much oil as possible. Let them sit for couple of minutes. Soak them in the hot syrup for 30 minutes before serving.

To serve, reheat by adding a little hot water to the syrup.

Note: The dough should be kneaded just enough so that a ball without cracks can be formed. Too much kneading is not necessary.

Kala Jamun
(Dark Brown Sweet Balls)

2 cups powdered whole milk
2 cups powdered nonfat milk
¼ teaspoon baking soda
¾ cup white flour
½ teaspoon ground cardamom
4 tablespoons of ghee, solidified
1½ cups crumbled panir
¾ cup half and half
8 cups sugar
9 cups water
4 cups oil for deep frying
1½ cups blanched ground almonds (optional)

In a large bowl, thoroughly mix the dry ingredients. Add the ghee and crumbled panir and blend with your fingers. Add the half and half gradually and keep working the mixture with your fingers. Add only enough half and half to make the mixture look like a dough; it may take the full 3/4 cup or a little less or a little more, depending on the moisture in the panir and the measuring of the dry ingredients.

When the mixture reaches the consistency of a soft dough, break off a piece and roll it into a walnut-size ball. If the ball is smooth, the dough is ready. If the mixture is too dry, it will not roll smoothly. Add a little more half and half as needed. Form all of the dough into balls; you will have 40 to 45 balls.

In a large saucepan, combine the sugar and water and bring to boil on medium high. Reduce the heat to medium low and continue cooking for about 10 minutes. Leave the syrup on low heat.

Heat oil for frying in a wok or heavy pan. To test the heat, drop a small piece of dough into the oil. It should rise to the surface immediately but should not turn dark. If it darkens, reduce the heat and let the temperature of the oil decrease before testing again. Put about 15-16 balls gently into the oil. As soon as they begin to float, stir and turn them gently to brown them on all sides. They will turn golden and then darken. Let them rest for 5 to 7 minutes and then put them in the hot syrup a few at a time, stirring gently. Let the jamuns sit in the syrup overnight.

Santosh Jain

Two hours before serving, take them out of the syrup. Roll them in the ground almonds and serve. If you do not wish to roll in almonds, just serve them at room temperature without syrup.

Kalakand
(Milk Cake)

(This is a dessert I always enjoyed back home. After a lot of experimentation, I have been able to achieve a reasonable version.)

1¼ cup powdered milk
2 tablespoons unsalted butter or 1 tablespoon ghee
16 ounces ricotta cheese
¾ cup sugar
4 tablespoons heavy cream
¾ teaspoon powdered cardamom
15-20 unsalted pistachios, finely chopped

In a dry skillet, heat the powdered milk on low for about 10 minutes, stirring constantly so that it is evenly roasted. The color should be a light pinkish tan. Put the milk in a bowl and reserve.

Heat the skillet on medium low. Add butter or ghee and ricotta cheese and stir for 5-6 minutes until the butter is melted and a little moisture evaporates. Add the sugar, heavy cream and powdered milk. Turn off the heat and stir in the cardamom.

Butter a 2-quart Pyrex dish and press the mixture into the dish with a rubber spatula. Microwave on high for 5 minutes. Stir and microwave for 3 minutes longer. Stir and microwave for about 2 minutes longer. The mixture should take on a pinkish color.

Sprinkle with chopped pistachios and press them in. Cool and cut into squares or diamond shapes to serve.

Gajjar Burfi

2 pounds carrots
2¾ cups sugar
4 tablespoons butter or 3 tablespoons ghee
1 teaspoon ground cardamom
Khoya made of 1 quart half and half and ½ gallon milk [Page xxii]
½ cup unsalted pistachios, finely chopped

Wash, peel and finely grate the carrots. Put carrots and sugar in a heavy, nonstick 12 inch skillet. Mix well and turn heat to medium high. Cook for 20 to 30 minutes, stirring occasionally to prevent carrots from burning, until the mixture dries. (Cooking time will vary with the moisture in the carrots.)

Add butter or ghee. Reduce the heat to medium and cook for 8 to 10 minutes longer. The carrots should look glazed.

Crumble the khoya and stir it into the carrots. Cook until khoya is completely blended into the carrots, about 10 minutes. Stir in the cardamom.

Grease a 9 x 13" cookie sheet. Pour the carrots into the cookie sheet and press down gently so that the mixture spreads evenly. Sprinkle with the pistachios and press them down with a spatula. Cool completely.

Cut into 1 ½ inch squares and store in an airtight container in the refrigerator. To serve, bring to room temperature.

Mohan Thal
(Milk and Gram Flour Fudge)

8 ounces unsalted butter
2 cups ladoo besan (coarse gram flour)
1 cup khoya (see recipe, page xxii)
1 teaspoon cardamom seeds
½ cup unsalted pistachio nuts, crushed

Syrup:
2 cups sugar
½ cup water
½ teaspoon yellow food coloring

To make syrup, put sugar and water in a 2 quart sauce pan on medium heat. Stir and cook until the sugar melts. Cook for about 10 minutes. Turn off the heat. The mixture should be syrupy. Add the food coloring and set aside.

Melt butter in a nonstick, heavy 12" skillet on medium. As soon as the butter has melted, add the gram flour and stir for 15 to 20 minutes or until you feel the gram flour becomes easy to stir, begins to darken and gives off a nice aroma. Add one-third of the khoya and stir for 5 minutes; add the remaining khoya, one-third at a time, and repeat. Add the crushed cardamom and continue until the gram flour turns pinkish brown.

Warm the syrup and add to the roasted gram flour. Stir vigorously for a couple of minutes. Remove from heat and pour the mixture into a 9 x 11" baking dish. Cool for 30 minutes. Sprinkle the crushed pistachios on top and press them in with a spatula. Cool completely (up to 6-8 hours). Cut into 1 1/4" squares. Store in an air tight container.

Keep refrigerated and bring to room temperature to serve.

Firni
(Custard Dessert)

½ cup long grain rice
¼ cup cold water
½ gallon whole milk
1 cup sugar
¾ cup half and half
1 teaspoon crushed cardamoms
a pinch of saffron soaked in a little milk
Slivered almonds and unsalted pistachio nuts

Soak the rice in cold water for 2-3 hours.

Pour water and milk into a heavy 4 -quart saucepan and place it on medium heat. It will take a while to come to the boil. If the milk is heated on medium and stirred off and on, it will not boil over and will not stick to the bottom of the pan. Once the milk comes to a boil, stir and cook for 10 to 15 minutes on medium heat.

Drain the rice and grind it in a blender, adding half and half gradually to make a smooth mixture.

Pour this mixture into the milk that has been cooking. As you pour, keep stirring to prevent lumps from forming. When the mixture thickens, which will happen very quickly, the firni should be cooking and it will take about 30 minutes for it to form bubbles and start cooking vigorously. Add the sugar, cardamom and saffron. As soon as the mixture reaches the consistency of a pudding, put it into a large bowl and let it cool. Refrigerate the pudding.

Garnish with the nuts and serve. This dessert can also be set and served in individual custard cups.

Note: *It is helpful to place a cake rack in between the pot and the stove.*

Ras Malai
(Panir Patties in a Creamy Sauce)

Panir made from 1/2 gallon milk
Seeds from 10 green cardamoms, crushed (3/4 teaspoon)
2 cups sugar (1½ cups for the syrup and ½ cup for the sauce)
6 cups water
1½ quarts half and half (½ cup for soaking the patties)
A pinch of saffron
½ cup sliced almonds
15 unsalted chopped pistachios

Crumble the panir and add the cardamom. Knead in electric mixer for about 5 minutes, or knead by hand until the dough is smooth and you can roll a piece of dough into a small ball without cracks. You should have a slight trace of fat on the palm of your hand after shaping a ball. Roll the rest of the panir into balls; you should have about 20. Flatten each ball into a patty approximately 1 1/2 inches in diameter and 3/8 inch thick.

Combine 1 1/2 cups sugar and water in a shallow 4-quart saucepan and boil for 5 minutes. Reduce the heat to medium high. Gently slide the patties into the syrup. When the syrup returns to the boil, reduce the heat to medium. Let the patties cook uncovered for half an hour. Sprinkle with cold water every 5 minutes. Cover the pot and turn the heat down to medium low and cook them for another 15 minutes. Let the patties cool down in the syrup for half an hour.

Mix the crushed saffron into 1/2 cup half and half. Gently remove the patties from the syrup and soak them in the half and half for 30 minutes.

Cook the remaining half and half for about 15 to 20 minutes on medium high stirring constantly, until it has been reduced by a little less than half. Stir in the remaining 1/2 cup sugar and cool. Add to the patties. Cover and refrigerate at least a day.

Garnish with the almonds and pistachios and serve.

Note: *This dish must be prepared at least a day ahead. Alternatively, you may prepare this dish a few days in advance, freeze it, and then thaw it in the refrigerator for a day and keep it at room temperature for a couple of hours before serving. It is also helpful to place a cake rack between the pot and the stove while reducing the half and half.*

Rice Kheer
(Rice Pudding)

½ cup water

½ gallon whole milk

¼ cup long grain rice soaked in cold water

¾ cup sugar (or to taste)

¾ teaspoon ground cardamom

¼ cup golden raisins (optional)

½ cup almonds, soaked in cold water overnight, peeled and slivered

2 tablespoons thinly sliced unsalted pistachios

In a deep, heavy pot pour in 1/4 cup cold water before adding milk. Turn heat to medium and bring the milk to a boil. (Do not heat the milk on high; the milk can burn before it boils.)

Wash and drain the soaked rice and add to the milk. Reduce the heat to medium low and stir the milk frequently. A layer of cream will form on the surface. Stir the milk each time this occurs to blend it in with the rest of the milk. Cook for about 45 minutes to an hour until the milk has cooked to a consistency thicker than heavy cream. The rice grains will cook and puff up and will seem to have multiplied miraculously.

Add the sugar, cardamom, raisins, and half of the almonds and cook, stirring, for another 5 minutes. Remove from the heat and put into a deep bowl to refrigerate. Serve chilled next day. Garnish with sliced almonds or pistachios.

Note: *To save the bottom of the pot from sticking, place a cake rack between the burner and the pot.*

Panir Ki Kheer
(Pudding with Panir)

Panir made from ½ gallon whole milk
¼ cup water
½ gallon whole milk
1 cup sugar
½ teaspoon crushed saffron
½ teaspoon crushed cardamom seeds
½ cup blanched slivered almonds or pistachios

Crumble the panir. A food processor with a rubber blade can be used for this step. Make sure there are no big pieces.

In a heavy 4-quart pot, add the water and then the milk. Cook on medium high, stirring occasionally. When the milk comes to a boil, add the crumbled panir and stir occasionally to ensure that a film does not form on top of the milk. If the milk boils up to the top of the pan, reduce the heat a little. However, kheer cooked on a lower heat takes on a pinkish-yellow color, rather than the preferred cream color.

Stir in the sugar, saffron and cardamom seeds and refrigerate until ready to serve.

Garnish with almonds, pistachios or both. The dessert may be served as is or with chopped fresh fruit, such as mangoes, strawberries, bananas, pineapple, grapes, etc.

Note: It is helpful to place a cake rack in between the pot and the stove.

Malai Pura
(Creamy Sweet Puffs)

2 cup half and half
½ cup whipping cream
1½ cup all purpose flour
½ teaspoon crushed cardamom seeds
2 to 2½ cup of cooking oil
1¼ cups sugar
½ cup of water
¼ cup slivered almonds
2 teaspoons unsalted pistachios, finely sliced

In a heavy saucepan or skillet (preferably nonstick), bring the half and half to a boil on medium high. Reduce the heat to medium. Stir and cook for about 10 minutes. Let the thickened milk cool down completely.

Whip the cream lightly and add the cooled half and half. Gradually add the flour, mixing all the flour into the half and half and beat well. Make sure that no lumps are formed. Add the crushed cardamoms. Let the mixture sit for an hour.

Heat the oil in a heavy skillet on medium heat. Drop a spoon of batter to test whether the oil is hot enough so that it does not burn but cooks gently. Now drop a tablespoon of batter in the oil. It should form into a small round pancake. Drop a few more. You may fry 5—6 at a time. Turn and cook them until they are a golden color. Drain on paper towels and place them in a dish in a single layer. Use up all the batter and make as many pancakes as you can.

In a saucepan, combine the water and sugar and bring to a boil. Reduce the heat and cook the syrup for 3—4 minutes. Pour the syrup over the puras (pancakes). Turn the puras so that they soak up the syrup. Sprinkle with slivered almond and pistachios.

Note: *You can make puras in advance, but add the hot syrup just before serving. That way, the puras will be served crisp.*

Appetizers

Appetizers or snacks are not an element in daily meals. Snacks are made whenever there is a festival celebration or served at formal meals. Snacks like *pakoras* or *samosas* are sometimes served when the family is together for a holiday or during monsoon weather, when people feel like eating something spicy and hot. Some snacks, like *mathri* or *namak pare,* are intended for between-meal snacking. Every region has its own favorite snacks. I have included a few recipes for you to try.

Mathri
(Crisp Rounds)

3 cups white flour
2 tablespoons semolina
1 teaspoon salt
¾ cup oil
1 teaspoon ajwain
¾ to 1 cup water
3 cups oil for deep frying

In a mixing bowl, combine flour, semolina, salt, oil and ajwain. Work the mixture with your fingers and it should have the texture of corn meal. Add the water gradually. The amount of water needed will depend on the temperature and the quality of the flour. The dough will form a ball but will still be crumbly; it should not be smooth. If the dough is smooth, make namak pare. (Recipe follows.) Let the dough rest, covered, about ten minutes.

Break off small pieces of dough and form it into balls about 1 - 1/2 inches in diameter. You should have about 50 balls. Roll each ball gently with a rolling pin to rounds 2 to 2 1/2 inches in diameter. The edges should be crumbly. Prick each mathri with the tip of a knife in 6 to 7 places.

Heat the oil on medium in a deep skillet or wok. Drop 8 to 10 mathris at a time into the hot oil. They should not turn color quickly. They should be cooked slowly and turn color gradually. They should not puff up. (That is why they are pricked.)

When the mathris turn pink and are crisp, take them out of the oil and drain on paper towels. Repeat until all the mathris are fried. Spread the cooked mathris out and let them cool completely. They can be kept in an airtight container for a month or so.

Masala Namak Pare
(Spicy Wafers)

(These spicy little snacks are excellent to serve with cocktails.)

2 cups white flour
2 tablespoons semolina
½ cup oil
½ teaspoon salt
²/³ to ¾ cup water
3 cups oil for deep frying

Masala:
½ teaspoon black pepper
½ teaspoon cayenne pepper
1 teaspoon amchur
½ teaspoon salt
1½ teaspoons cumin seeds, dry roasted and ground

Mix together flour, semolina, oil and salt. Rub the mixture with your fingers until it feels like cornmeal. Add the water gradually and knead. The dough should be smooth and stiff. Let the dough rest for 10 to 20 minutes. Divide it into three or four parts. Roll the dough on a wooden board to 1/8 inch thickness. Cut into strips about 1/3 to 1/2" wide. Now cut the strips crosswise to make 1/2 inch squares or diamonds.

Heat the oil in a wok or deep skillet on medium heat. Scrape the namak pare from the board with a spatula and drop them in the oil. Stir them gently. They should slowly turn a pinkish gold color. Take them out of the oil and drain on a paper towel. Repeat until all the namak pare are fried.

Place all the namak pare in a brown paper bag and sprinkle the mixed masala over them. Close the bag and shake it until all the namak pare are coated with the spices.

Cool completely and store in an airtight container.

Note: *Namak pare can be made without the masala.*

Palak Ki Tikki
(Deep-fried Spinach Patties)

1 cup yellow split peas
1½ cups boiled potatoes, grated
2 cups fresh spinach, finely chopped
½ cup onion, finely chopped
1 or 2 green chilies, finely chopped
1 teaspoon cumin seeds
2 teaspoons crushed coriander seeds
1 teaspoon garam masala
1 teaspoon salt
3 cups oil for deep frying

Soak the split peas in cold water at least 4 hours. Wash and drain them and grind them with 1/4 cup water. In a big bowl, whip the split peas for 2 to 3 minutes. Stir in the remaining ingredients except the oil and mix well. Form the mixture into small patties about 1 1/2 inches in size. You will have about 30 patties.

Heat the oil in a wok on medium high. Test the temperature by dropping a little piece of the mixture into the oil. If it rises quickly to the top, the oil is ready. When the oil is hot, add the patties a few at a time. Turn them over and over and fry until they are golden brown. You may have to turn them a couple of times.

Note: *If the oil is not hot enough, the patties will spread out and lose their shape.*

Sabzi Pakoras
(Vegetable fritters)

2 pounds vegetables (potatoes, onions, eggplant, zucchini, bell peppers, cauliflower and broccoli)
2 cups gram flour
1 cup water
1 teaspoon salt
¼ to ½ teaspoon cayenne pepper
½ teaspoon ground cumin
½ teaspoon ground coriander
½ teaspoon garam masala
2 tablespoons yogurt
Oil for deep frying

Slice potatoes and onions about 1/4 inch thick. Slice eggplant and zucchini into 1/4"rounds. Slice the bell peppers into1-2" slices. Cut cauliflower and broccoli into 2" florets. Sprinkle the vegetables with a little salt and cayenne pepper and leave them in a colander to drain.

About an hour before cooking, mix the flour and water in a large bowl. When you are ready to cook the pakoras, add all the spices and the yogurt and beat the mixture well to make a batter.

Heat the oil to smoking in a deep frying pan or a wok. Reduce the heat to medium. Dip a piece of vegetable in the batter. Shake off the extra batter and carefully slide the vegetables into the oil from the side of the wok or pan to avoid splattering. Fry only a few pieces at a time, turning them frequently until they are golden brown. Drain them on paper towels and serve hot with mint chutney.

Alu Palak Pakora
(Fritters with Spinach and Potatoes)

2 cups spinach, washed and finely chopped
1 cup coarsely chopped onion
1 cup peeled diced potatoes
2 jalapeños, finely chopped
2 teaspoons salt
2 cup gram flour
1 teaspoon amchur or 1 tablespoon lemon juice
2 teaspoons coriander seed
1 teaspoon cumin seeds
1 teaspoon garam masala
3 cups vegetable oil for deep frying

In a large bowl, combine the spinach, onion, potatoes, jalapeños, gram flour and salt. Mix well, cover and let the mixture rest for an hour. It will release a lot of moisture. Add the remaining spices and mix well.

Heat the oil in a wok on medium high. To test, drop a little of the mixture into the oil. It should start floating quickly without turning dark brown.

Spoon the mixture into the oil, I tablespoon at a time. You can cook 10 to 12 spoonfuls at a time. When the pakoras float in the oil, turn them constantly so that they cook evenly on all sides to a golden brown. Drain on paper towels.

Repeat until all the pakoras are cooked. This quantity of batter will make 40 to 45 pakoras.

Samosa

Pastry:
2 cups all-purpose flour

6 tablespoons oil

½ teaspoon salt

½ cup cold water

Filling:
4 tablespoons oil

2 teaspoons coriander seeds

1 teaspoon cumin seeds

4 cups potatoes, diced

1 tablespoon ginger, finely chopped

1 to 1½ teaspoons salt

½ cup green peas

1 or 2 green chilies, chopped

1 teaspoon ground cumin

2 teaspoons ground coriander

2 teaspoons amchur or lime juice

1 teaspoon garam masala

3 tablespoons flour

¼ cup water or enough to make a paste to seal the samosas

About 3 cups oil for deep frying

In a large bowl, mix the flour, salt and oil with your fingers. Add the water gradually and mix it in to form a dough. (Caution: Do not add the water all at once.) Knead the dough until it is smooth. Place it in a covered bowl and let it rest for 20 to 30 minutes.

Heat the oil in a large skillet. When it is hot, add the coriander seeds and cumin seeds. When the seeds are sizzling, add the potatoes, ginger and salt. Mix them well, cover and cook on medium low for 6 to 7 minutes. When the potatoes are a little tender, add the peas and chilies and ground coriander and cumin. Cook the mixture uncovered for about 10 minutes, stirring frequently to mix the spices into the vegetables.

Add the amchur and garam masala. Mix well. Turn off the heat and let the filling cool.

Make a paste of the flour and water to seal the samosas. Divide the dough into 12 portions. Form each portion into a smooth ball. Roll one ball into a 5 to 6 inch round. Cut the round in half. Apply the flour and water paste to one half of the straight edge. Pick up one edge and press it to the side with the paste to form a cone. Make a circle with your thumb and index finger. Let the cone sit on the circle of your thumb and index finger. (**See illustration.**) Place a tablespoon of the filling in the cone. Apply paste to the inside edges of the filled cone and seal it by pinching the edges together. Fill all the half-rounds with the filling and seal them.

Heat the oil to medium hot in a heavy pan. To test the temperature, drop in a crumb of dough. It should rise to the top immediately. Slide in 5 to 6 samosas, one at a time. Turn them with a slotted spoon or spatula so that they fry evenly and take on a light golden color. Drain on paper towels to soak up the excess oil. Serve hot with coriander chutney and mint chutney.

Note: Samosas can be prepared in advance. Fry them until they are half cooked. Cool, wrap tightly and freeze. To serve, thaw and bake in a 325° oven for 1 hour.

STEPS FOR MAKING SAMOSA

1

2

3

4

5

6

STEPS FOR MAKIANG ALU TIKKI

1

2

3

4

5

Alu Tikki
(Potato Patties)

6 large potatoes
2 slices bread
1 teaspoon salt
½ teaspoon cayenne pepper

Boil the potatoes in salted water until tender. Cool completely, peel and grate the potatoes. Soak the bread in water for about 10 minutes. Squeeze all the water out of the bread and mix the bread with the potatoes. Add the salt and cayenne and set aside.

Filling:
1 tablespoon oil
¾ teaspoon cumin seeds
1½ tablespoons minced fresh ginger
1 teaspoon ground cumin
1 teaspoon ground coriander
½ teaspoon cayenne
½ teaspoon salt
2 cups frozen peas
1 teaspoon amchur or 1 tablespoon lemon juice
¼ cup chopped cilantro
1 green chili, finely chopped (optional)
Spray oil for frying

Heat 1 tablespoon oil in a skillet over medium heat. Add the cumin seeds. As soon as they begin to sizzle, stir in the ginger, cumin, coriander and cayenne. Add the salt and peas and stir the mixture for a couple of minutes. Cover and cook for 5-7 minutes or until the peas are tender. Mash the peas until they are about half crushed and add the amchur or lemon juice. Add the chopped cilantro and chili and remove from the heat.

Divide the potato mixture into 40 walnut-size balls. Divide the filling into 20 equal portions. Grease your palms and flatten two potato balls into 3-3 ½" patties. Put one portion of filling on one patty and cover with the second patty. Pinch the edges all the way

189

around and pat down the filled patty slightly. Repeat the process until all potato balls and filling are used up.

Heat a large griddle on medium. Spray generously with oil. Place patties on the griddle and spray the top with additional oil. Fry the patties until golden and crispy on one side; turn and cook the other side.

Serve hot with mint coriander chutney and tamarind chutney.

Moong ke Shami Kabob
(Vegetarian Kabob)

1 inch cinnamon stick
3—4 whole cloves
5—6 green cardamoms
7—8 black peppercorns
2 bay leaves
1 cup whole moong dal
1½ cups water
2—3 cloves of garlic
1 tablespoon minced ginger
1 teaspoon salt
½ teaspoon cayenne
4 medium potatoes
1 teaspoon ground cumin
1 teaspoon ground coriander
1 teaspoon garam masala
2 teaspoons amchur or lemon juice
1 green chili, finely chopped
2 tablespoons cilantro, finely chopped

For batter:
2 tablespoons flour
2 tablespoons yogurt
¾ cup water
½ teaspoon salt
¼ teaspoon cayenne pepper

For garnish:
1 small sweet or red onion
1 small tomato
1 lime, sliced into thin rounds

Tie up the whole spices in a small square of muslin.

Pick over, wash and soak whole moong in water for 4—5 hours. Drain the moong and put it in a heavy based saucepan. Add minced ginger, garlic, salt, red chili and the bag of whole spices and bring to a boil on medium high. When the dal begins to boil rapidly, turn the heat down to medium low; cover the saucepan and simmer for about 20 minutes. Check to be sure the beans are very tender and mushy. Raise the heat to evaporate excess moisture, if necessary. If the moong is not mushy, add a little water and cook a little longer. Once the moong is cooked, let it cool.

Peel and grate the boiled potatoes. Remove the pouch of whole spices and mash the moong. Mix the potatoes into the mashed moong along with green chilies, salt, cilantro, ground cumin and coriander, garam masala and amchur or lemon juice.

Form the mixture into small patties (30 to 35 patties, depending upon the size). Whisk the yogurt, flour and half of the water. Slowly add the remaining water while continuing to whisk. Add salt and pepper.

Heat a griddle on medium heat. Spread a bit of oil on the griddle. Dip each patty in the batter and place it on the hot griddle. You can cook 8 to10 patties at a time. Turn and drizzle a little oil around the patties. Both sides should become golden and crusty. Repeat the process until all the patties are done.

Garnish with onion, tomatoes and lemon slices and serve with mint chutney.

Note: *The sliced onions can be soaked in ice water for half an hour. They become crisp and sweet.*

Alu Bonda
(Spiced Potato Balls)

3 large or 4 medium Yukon potatoes (5—5½ cups)
2 tablespoons coriander seeds
1 teaspoon cumin seeds
½ teaspoon ajwain (optional)
2 teaspoons salt
2 teaspoons amchur or 1 tablespoon lemon juice
1 teaspoon garam masala
1 green chili, finely chopped
1 tablespoon minced ginger
½ cup finely chopped cilantro
1½ cups gram flour (Besan)
1 teaspoon salt
½ teaspoon cayenne pepper (optional)
1 teaspoon ground cumin
1 teaspoon ground coriander
2 tablespoons yogurt
¾ cup water
2½ to 3 cups vegetable or peanut oil for deep frying

Boil the potatoes in salted water. Let them cool down completely. Grate them with a coarse grater. You should have 5 to 5½ cups, loosely packed. Mix in all the spices, green chili, ginger and cilantro.

Form the mixture into golf ball sized balls. Flatten them a little. You should have 20 to 25 patties.

In a mixing bowl, add the gram flour, salt, cayenne, ground cumin and ground coriander. Mix well and add yogurt. Gradually whisk in the water. The batter should be the consistency of egg whites. Let it sit for 30 minutes.

Heat the oil in a wok on medium heat. Test by dropping in a drop of batter. If it comes up to the top of the oil surface, it is ready. Pick up one patty at a time. Dip in the batter; shake off the excess batter and gently slide it into the oil. You should be able to fry 6 to 7 patties at one time. Once, they start floating, turn them over and fry until they turn golden in color. You may have to turn them over a couple of times.

Drain and place them on a paper towel. Repeat with the rest of the patties until they are all fried. Serve them hot with mint and coriander chutney.

Chutneys, Pickles, Salads and Relishes

Chutneys, pickles and salads commonly appear on Indian tables as condiments and may accompany any meal. Certain kinds of chutneys are customarily served with specific dishes. Samosas, for example, must be served with mint, coriander and tamarind chutneys to be complete.

Pickles and relishes are often made with seasonal vegetables. I include a few examples for you to try.

Salads in India are served with a simple dressing of salt, black pepper and lime juice. The diner enjoys a small quantity of salad, not the big bowl of mixed vegetables with salad dressing that Americans are accustomed to.

Apple Chutney

4 cups cooking apples, unpeeled, cored and grated
1½ cups sugar
½ cup vinegar
6 to 8 green cardamoms
2 teaspoons fennel seeds
1 teaspoon black pepper corns
1 cinnamon stick
1/2 teaspoon crushed red chilies
1 teaspoon salt
1/2 cup raisins

Stir the sugar and vinegar into the grated apples and cook the mixture on low heat for about 10 minutes. Crush the spices and stir them into the apples. Stir in the salt and raisins. Stir the mixture occasionally to prevent burning on the bottom. Cook the apples for 10 minutes; add the spices and cook for 2 more minutes. When the apples change color and a glaze appears on the chutney, turn off the heat. Cool the chutney and pack it in clean jars. Refrigerated, it will keep for four to six weeks.

Note: *Use the vinegar if the apples are sweet. If they are tart, omit the vinegar.*

Mango Chutney

4 large unripe mangoes, peeled and grated (about 8 cups)

2 cups sugar

10 cloves

3" inch cinnamon stick

1½ teaspoons peppercorns

1 teaspoon crushed red chili

½ teaspoon crushed cardamom seeds

2 teaspoons salt

Crush or coarsely grind the whole spices. In a large skillet, combine the mangoes with the remaining ingredients. Cook on medium, stirring constantly. When half the liquid has evaporated, reduce the heat to low and simmer about 30 minutes until the juice becomes syrupy and the chutney appears glazed. Cool; place in jars. This chutney will keep for about two months in the refrigerator.

Santosh Jain

Mint and Cilantro Chutney

1 cup fresh mint, loosely packed
2 cups cilantro, leaves and tender stems, coarsely chopped
1 cup scallions, coarsely chopped
3 to 4 green chilies
½ cup freshly squeezed lime juice
1 to 1½ teaspoons salt
2 teaspoons cumin seed, roasted
½ cup water

Put all the ingredients into a blender or food processor and grind to a fine paste. Refrigerate until ready to serve.

Pineapple and Apricot Chutney

8 ounces dried apricots
20 ounce can crushed pineapple in its own juice
1½ to 2 teaspoons salt
¾ cup sugar
½ to 1 teaspoon crushed red pepper
2 teaspoons crushed fennel seeds
½ teaspoon crushed cardamom seeds
½ cup slivered almonds (optional)

Wash the apricots and cook them in 1 cup water for about 10 minutes on medium low. The apricots should absorb all the liquid and be tender. Mash or finely chop the cooked apricots. Stir in the remaining ingredients and cook on medium low for 30-35 minutes until the chutney looks glazed. Cool and place in jars. This chutney will keep, refrigerated, for up to two months.

Add the slivered almonds after the chutney is cooked.

Sweet and Sour Tamarind Chutney

5 ounces tamarind
2 cups hot water
¾ cup brown sugar
1 teaspoon salt
½ teaspoon crushed red chilies
1 teaspoon garam masala
1 teaspoon cumin seeds, roasted and ground

Soak the tamarind in the hot water for about four hours. When it is soft, mash it with your fingers to extract all the pulp. Strain the pulp through a colander.

In a saucepan, combine the tamarind pulp, brown sugar, salt and chilies. Cook on medium 15 to 20 minutes. Add the garam masala and the cumin seeds. Cool and refrigerate. Refrigerated, this chutney will keep for about a month.

Note: *Tamarind comes in 10 ounce slabs. Use half a slab.*

Gajjar Ka Achar
(Carrot Pickle)

1 pound carrots
¾ teaspoon crushed red pepper
¾ teaspoon paprika or cayenne pepper
1 tablespoon finely crushed black mustard seeds
½ teaspoon turmeric
1 tablespoon sea salt
½ teaspoon garam masala
1/3 cup mustard oil
Pinch asafetida
¼ cup fresh lime juice

Wash and scrape the carrots. Cut them into pieces measuring 2" x 1/2" x 1/2". Put them on paper towels for about 30 minutes.

Put the carrots into a ceramic or glass bowl and add all the spices and salt. Mix well and let the carrots sit for about 10 minutes.

Heat the oil in a nonstick skillet on medium high. Add the mustard oil and heat until it is smoking. Remove from the heat and add asafetida and carrot mixture. Reduce the heat to medium and return the skillet to the stove. Stir the carrots to coat them with the oil. Stir and cook the carrots until they are just tender but still a little crunchy. Turn off the heat.

Cool the carrots and put them into a sterilized jar. When they have completely cooled down, cover and let them sit on the counter. Shake the jar every so often. Keep the jar on the counter for three days.

The pickle may be eaten immediately or stored, refrigerated, for 8-10 days.

Khata Meetha Neembu Ka Achar
(Sweet and Sour Lime Pickle)

1 pound limes
¼ cup sea salt
¼ cup sugar
¾ cup sugar
2 tablespoon crushed black pepper
¾ teaspoon ground cinnamon
½ teaspoon ground ginger powder
½ teaspoon ground cloves

Wash and dry the limes. Cut them into 1/8" slices. Put the slices into a glass bowl and add the salt, sugar and spices. Mix well and put mixture into a sterilized jar. Cover the jar and shake well. Put the jar out in the sun for three to four days and then keep it on the counter for a couple of weeks. As time passes, the skin of the limes becomes tender and does not taste bitter. You can keep this pickle in the refrigerator for a year.

Neembu, Mirchi aur Adrak Ka Achar
(Lemon, Green Chili and Ginger Pickle)

1 teaspoon ajwain
1 pound lemons
¼ cup sea salt
1 teaspoon crushed red pepper
8 green chilies
¼ cup sliced ginger

Dry roast the ajwain until it is two shades darker.

Wash the lemons and put them on a paper towel. Let them dry for a couple of hours and then wipe them with a dry dish cloth. Cut the lemons into halves and then halves again. You will have four pieces. Cut each piece in half again. You will have eight pieces.

Put the lemons into a glass or ceramic bowl and add the ajwain, salt and crushed pepper. Mix thoroughly and put the mixture into a sterilized jar. Put a muslin piece on the mouth of the jar and cover it with the lid. Put the jar in the sun and shake the pickle two to three times a day. After a couple of days, wash and dry the green chilies and cut them into 2-3 pieces.

Scrape the ginger and cut it into 1" x 1/4" slices. Leave the ginger out to dry on paper towels. (Before you add the ginger to the pickle, make sure it is totally dry.) Add the chilies and ginger to the pickle.

Leave the jar in the sun for another two to three days and then leave it on the counter for another week or ten days. The chilies and ginger can be eaten immediately, but the lemons will take another week to 10 days to be ready to eat.

This pickle can be kept refrigerated for a year.

Alu Ka Achar
(Potato Pickle)

1 pound potatoes
2 fresh bright red chilies or 1 teaspoon cayenne pepper
4 tablespoons lemon juice
1 cup vegetable oil
2 tablespoons mustard oil
Small pinch asafetida
¾ teaspoon fenugreek seeds
1 teaspoon fennel seeds
1 teaspoon salt

Parboil the potatoes and cool. Cut them into 3/4" pieces. Grind chilies and mix them into the lemon juice.

Heat the vegetable oil in a heavy skillet or small wok on medium high. When the oil is hot, fry the potato pieces. They should be crusty and golden in color. Drain the potato pieces and set them aside on paper towels.

Heat the mustard oil on medium high in the wok or skillet. Add the asafetida and the fenugreek and fennel seeds, cayenne pepper and salt. Stir and add the potatoes, chilies and lemon juice. Cook on medium until the sauce wraps around the potatoes. Turn the heat off and cool the pickle completely. Put it into a sterilized pint jar and refrigerate.

This pickle is ready to eat immediately and can be kept 5-6 days in the refrigerator. It taste the best when freshly prepared.

Sprouted Whole Moong Dal Salad

This salad can be served as a light meal.

2 cups whole moong dal
1 tablespoon vegetable oil
1 teaspoon whole cumin seeds
¼ cup chopped fresh ginger
½ teaspoon turmeric
1½ teaspoons salt
2 cups water
2 cups chopped fresh tomatoes
2 cups boiled potatoes, cut in 1/2 inch cubes
1 or 2 green jalapeño peppers, optional
1 cup fresh cilantro, chopped
1 medium red or sweet onion, finely diced
4 tablespoons fresh lime or lemon juice
1½ teaspoons roasted ground cumin seed
1 teaspoon garam masala

Wash and soak the moong dal in 8 cups lukewarm water for 8—12 hours. Drain and put in a wet muslin cloth for another 12 to 24 hours, depending upon the weather. The moong dal will split open and should sprout just a bit.

In a large, heavy skillet, heat the oil on medium heat. Add the cumin seeds. They should sizzle and darken. Add the chopped fresh ginger. Sauté for 2 minutes and then add the turmeric, sprouted dal and salt. Stir and mix well to coat the beans with oil and spices. Add water.

Turn heat to high and bring to a boil, uncovered. Turn heat to low and cook, covered. Stir after 4—5 minutes. Cover and cook for 15 to 20 minutes.

Put the cooked beans in a large serving bowl and cool. Be sure the beans have cooled to room temperature before adding ingredients in List 2, above. If you add these ingredients when the beans are still hot, they will cook with the heat and the salad will not taste fresh and crisp.

Note: *Beans sprout in less time when the weather is hot. During colder weather they take longer. On a hot, humid day, the beans may sprout in 12 hours instead of 24. You will need to check and cook them when they have sprouted just a bit.*

Kachumbar
(Onion, Tomato and Cucumber Salad)

1 medium size sweet or red onion
1 cucumber, peeled and chopped
1 large tomato, chopped
1 small green chili (optional)
¼ cup cilantro, minced
1 teaspoon salt
¾ teaspoon crushed black pepper
2 tablespoons lime juice

Chop the onions in small chunks and soak them in iced water for about 1/2 hour. Drain the onions and mix with cucumber and tomato. Finely chop the green chili and mix it with the vegetables; add the cilantro.

You can make the salad ahead of time and refrigerate it. Add salt, pepper and lime juice, and mix well before serving.

Carrot Salad

2 cups carrots
1 teaspoon oil
½ teaspoon mustard seeds
2 green chilies, finely chopped
½ teaspoon salt
1 teaspoon sugar
2 tablespoon lime juice

Grate the carrots.

Heat the oil in a skillet on medium. Add the mustard seeds. As soon as they start to splatter, add the carrots, green chilies, salt and sugar.

Mix well and cook, covered, for 2-3 minutes.

Remove from heat and stir in the lime juice. Serve at room temperature.

Onion Relish

2 medium red or sweet onions
1 teaspoon salt
½ teaspoon paprika
2 tablespoons lemon or lime juice

Cut the onions in thin long slices. Soak the onions in ice water for at least 30 minutes. Drain thoroughly. In a bowl, mix the drained onions, salt, paprika and lemon or lime juice. Mix it and serve. This relish goes especially very well with chickpea dishes.

Radish or Daikon Relish

1 pound radishes or daikon
1 teaspoon ajwain, dry roasted until it is two shades darker
1 green chili, finely chopped (optional)
1 teaspoon salt
2-3 tablespoons lime juice

Grate the radishes or daikon in a food processor, using a medium grater plate. Put the grated radishes or daikon in a bowl. Add ajwain, green chilies, salt and lime juice. Mix well and serve.

Index of Recipes
(English Titles)

Printed in the United States
19319LVS00002B/3-6

9 781414 009162